PRAISE FOR *E*

"In this brief, story-driven book, Mark L. Yackel-Juleen creates bridges across the many familiar divides we inhabit. *Everyone Must Eat* offers a way past urban/rural, foodie/corporation, libertarian/government activist and draws us into the complexities of living in deep relationship with each other and all of creation. An excellent read. I highly recommend it!"

—Mary Hess, professor of educational leadership
and chair of the leadership division, Luther Seminary

"Ending hunger and building a sustainable food system for the future means confronting the structures, policies, and institutions that shape how we get our food. But this also means understanding the communities, cultures, and history of our relationship to food, land, and people. Yackel-Juleen reminds us that behind heady topics such as sustainability and efficiency are deeper issues of value, meaning, identity, faith, and vocation. He deftly bridges his personal experience with data to uncover the realities behind our current food system and what we need to change for the future. His careful research, deep reflection on faith, and practical tips for ministry bring readers into the lives and histories of rural communities that are too often overlooked. As Yackel-Juleen writes, it is the story of the 'land and the people' that reminds us that ending hunger is about 'relationships, not just the economics of global food production.' That is an important reminder, and the book should be required reading for anyone passionate about food, hunger, the environment, and the future of the church."

—Ryan P. Cumming, program director of hunger
education for ELCA World Hunger and senior
lecturer at Loyola University Chicago's School
of Continued and Professional Studies

"Mark Yackel-Juleen's clear-eyed reckoning that we need 'to accomplish a more just food system and maintain a healthier planet' emerges from careful listening and faithful service among rural people. In a society desperately groping for meaningful response to climate disaster, *Everyone Must Eat* offers ways to replace hand-wringing with hands-on expression of God's abiding love for God's good creation."

—Gilson Waldkoenig, PhD, Paulssen-Hale-Maurer
Professor of Church in Society and director
of the Town and Country Church Institute
for United Lutheran Seminary, Gettysburg
and Philadelphia, Pennsylvania

"*Everyone Must Eat* is a book for our time, confronting widespread misunderstanding about the relationship between food and the cultural, theological, and sociological context of rural people and places. Yackel-Juleen's book is a resource for training and equipping readers to engage reflectively with the 'agri-culture' of rural areas. His passion for rural ministry threads its way through this book, encouraging people to embrace a calling to love the people and places that are often overshadowed or marginalized by corporations and national or global priorities in food production."

—Heather J. Major, Highland Theological College;
PhD in practical theology, rural church,
and mission, University of Glasgow

"*Everyone Must Eat* is a thumbs-up, and I highly endorse it. It is well written, easy to read, and full of great information. While writing primarily for leaders of rural or small-town congregations, Yackel-Juleen offers helpful ideas for any professional who wants to understand how to work most effectively with rural people."

—David Ruesink, professor emeritus,
Texas A&M University; executive secretary,
Rural Church Network of the United States and Canada;
treasurer, International Rural Chaplains Association;
and North American representative,
International Rural Churches Association

"*Everyone Must Eat* offers an excellent primer about everything rural. A great resource, especially for pastors new to ministry in rural communities."

—Dr. Bernie Evans, professor emeritus at Saint John's
University, Collegeville, Minnesota, where he taught
courses on Christian social ethics, environmental
theology, and ministry in rural communities;
author of *Glorify the Lord by Your Life: Catholic
Social Teaching and the Liturgy* (2020) and *Lazarus
at the Table: Catholics and Social Justice* (2006)

Everyone Must Eat

Everyone Must Eat

Everyone Must Eat

Food, Sustainability, and Ministry

Mark L. Yackel-Juleen

Fortress Press

Minneapolis

EVERYONE MUST EAT
Food, Sustainability, and Ministry

Scripture quotations are from the New Revised Standard Version Bible
© 1989 Division of Christian Education of the National Council of the
Churches of Christ in the United States of America. Used by permission.

Cover Image: © iStock 2018, Working hard stock photo by warrengoldswan
Cover Design: Alisha Lofgren

Print ISBN: 978-1-5064-4838-1
eBook ISBN: 978-1-5064-4839-8

CONTENTS

INTRODUCTION

Across the picnic table sat one of the preeminent environmental theologians of the 1970s and 1980s. He was Rev. Dr. Richard Cartwright Austin, a Presbyterian minister, an author, and an activist. He cochaired a coalition that resulted in then president Jimmy Carter signing the Surface Mining Control and Reclamation Act of 1977—an effort to protect Appalachian environments and small communities. The issue that had driven him from minister to environmental activist was mountaintop removal mining (MTR), the practice of literally removing a mountaintop to access the coal beneath. The process was cheaper for the coal companies and, they argued, safer for miners than underground mining. But the detrimental impact on the environment and the communities around MTR sites was substantial. There was no legal requirement for the coal companies to restore or "reclaim" the environments and communities that had been devastated by this practice. And so Rev. Dr. Austin engaged the issue on behalf of the people and place he had come to love and serve. My spouse and I were attending the Washington Island Forum, a continuing education event in Door County, Wisconsin. The theme was "Care of Creation," and Dr. Austin was the keynote speaker. I was an inexperienced, newly ordained pastor.

But my spouse and I were also wrestling with how to faithfully understand and engage outside forces that were adversely impacting the community and place we were called to serve, though in a different context. Perhaps Dr. Austin could offer some guidance. When I was a seminary student, the general understanding among my classmates was that rural ministry was a stepping-stone, a minor league preparation for a better call. You would serve two or three years in a small rural parish and work your way up to a larger, preferably metropolitan congregation where the "real" ministry happened. When I was ordained in 1989, I was called to serve two small congregations in southwestern Minnesota and settled into a community of one hundred people. It was the time of the "farm crisis." It quickly became apparent we were living in and serving a community that was being devastated by emerging global economic and demographic change, particularly in the food system. There were farm foreclosures, bank failures, suicides and attempted suicides, and even the murder of two bankers in a small town and the suicide of the "failed" dairy farmer who shot them. It was a time when small communities and the congregations that served them feared for their survival. It was a crisis indeed. I soon realized that this wasn't minor league ministry, and my spouse and I felt engaged with and committed to the people and the land.

Then we began to dream. How could we help others experience the importance of these realities and commit to mission and ministry in a rural context, not as a stepping-stone, but as a valid missional calling? What if we created a place on a farm site where community leaders could gather and grapple with these issues on common ground? It could be a place where future church leaders come and learn about these issues firsthand. It could be a place for people to reflect on mission, ministry, and shalom amid the turmoil of economic, demographic, and environmental change—globally and locally.

After listening to our dream, Dr. Austin looked up from his paper plate of brats, beans, and potato salad and said, "The people in the rural communities you serve are on the front lines of perhaps the most crucial global issues now that the Cold War is not an imminent danger—environmental sustainability and food production. I think you should go for it." I wrote those words down. That was 1991. The Berlin Wall had just come down. The concept of global warming and climate change was just entering public consciousness. But the economic impacts of a globalizing and consolidating food system reverberated right down to small, rural communities and even the very soil itself. These realities have deep biblical and theological implications. Thus was conceived, in 1992, a place called Shalom Hill Farm, a retreat and educational ministry on a farm site in southwestern Minnesota. And thus began a very steep learning curve for me as a local theologian and founder of a nonprofit organization.

The issues surrounding food production and their impact on land and community are not just rural concerns because, as this book's title asserts, *Everyone Must Eat*. The Anglican Old Testament scholar and ethicist Christopher J. H. Wright states in his book *God's People in God's Land*, "All that we can count as material goods originates from what grows on, feeds on, or is dug out of the soil of our planet. Even in our modern industrial and highly technological world, we depend on the efficient use of well-maintained farmland to keep us fed and clothed while we go about our creation and consumption of wealth in other ways many steps removed from direct contact with the land."[1] How food is produced and the environmental and economic sustainability of the food system are primary concerns for those who tend the creation. For food producers, environmentalists, and conservationists, these are matters of livelihood, vocation, and often passionate ethical concern. But these are also vital issues for all of human society and, in truth, all of God's creatures and creation. They pertain to seed, genes, soil, water, and air—the seminal components needed to sustain life. Sustainability and survival are inextricably interdependent. The ongoing survival of species, human or otherwise, is predicated on sustainability. My mentor Dr. C. Dean Freudenberger frequently stresses that sustainability is a matter of transgenerational justice, global concerns not just for this generation but for generations to come.

I have been challenged to engage these issues throughout my ministry—locally, nationally, and globally. As a local parish pastor, I witnessed parishioners who worked hard to produce food in the best way they could while balancing the need for financial viability and care for the land. I also witnessed professional conservationists, soil scientists, ecosystem hydrologists, and prairie botanists fight for ecosystem sustainability via public policy and boots on the land. In my involvement with the rural movement of the Evangelical Lutheran Church in America (ELCA), these issues were front and center for regionally based organizations like the Great Plains Coalition for Rural Ministry and the Region 3 Rural Leadership Conference. On an international level, in my leadership roles in the Rural Church Network of the United States and Canada and the International Rural Churches Association, I see these issues through a much broader lens. While serving as a lay missionary teacher in Hong Kong in the 1980s, I was first drawn into environmental/community activism related to the establishment of a nuclear power plant. It was located upwind from the Kowloon Peninsula, one of the most densely populated places on the planet, without an evacuation plan required by international nuclear regulations. It was then that I became involved with Friends of the Earth, an international environmental advocacy organization, seeking answers to big questions from powerful international players.

In writing this book, I stand on the shoulders of many astute scholars, some of whom have been my teachers and mentors either in the classroom or through their writings or personal guidance. I have already introduced you to some—Richard Cartwright Austin, Christopher J. H. Wright, and C. Dean Freudenberger—and I will make more introductions in the chapters that follow. Many of these scholars were prescient, some might say prophetic, in their stressing the urgency of this topic. This book seeks to build on what has gone before but with a twenty-first-century perspective and a practical ministry application. My intention is that a seminarian who is going to serve in a rural context reads this book and becomes better equipped to serve in that context. My intention is that a pastor or other church leader who wants to deepen their understanding of the connections between biblical/theological tradition and the current realities of food production and sustainability reads this book and is enriched and better informed. My intention is that a teaching theologian or pastor who wants a resource for a course on this general topic reads this book and finds the most accessible and current treatment of the subject. That is why questions for either individual reflection or group discussion are included at the end of each chapter. The recommended resources section is also an instrument for deeper learning.

The reader will note an abundance of stories throughout the book. This introduction began with a story through which I sought to convey something of who I am and why I am passionate about this topic. I have discovered in my years of ministry that narrative is the most effective way to engage others in reflection and conversation about important and often conflictual topics. For this insight into the significance of story in rural communities, I owe a deep debt of gratitude to a little book by Rev. Dr. Tex Sample with the colorful title *Ministry in an Oral Culture: Living with Will Rogers, Uncle Remus, and Minnie Pearl.* Here is another introduction I gladly make. In Sample's work, I discovered a remarkable description of the cultural context in which I was serving, a context where a well-told story can open a window to refreshing discussion and theological reflection. And story is the foundation of our biblical tradition. I have been captivated by the biblical narrative—God's word. I seek to demonstrate the power of story and encourage you, the reader, to tell stories.

In chapter 1, I will identify issues related to food production and environmental sustainability, many of which are as current as the daily news. I will also point to some behind-the-scenes realities of which the general public is not aware—realities with which food producers grapple and that the ministers who serve them should understand.

In chapter 2, I will explore some of the unique sociological dynamics of rural communities, especially those related to food production. In rural settings, there is an intimate relationship between land/creation, economy, and community that is often multigenerational. Rural life is highly relational. As already mentioned, it is a culture where orality and narrative are key, especially for the new immigrants who are populating many rural communities to work in food production or processing. A leader in such a context seeking to engage the issues in chapter 1 would benefit by attending to these sociological dynamics. But it is also true that these communities include folks who are first- or second-generation residents displaced from the land. As a metro church leader, you might be serving people who have been displaced from rural contexts. They come with this rural sociological formation. They come with memory. You will be better for recognizing and honoring this background. This chapter will name some of the more salient sociological nuances, supported by research.

Chapter 3 will connect biblical and theological concepts with the issues named in chapter 1 and the sociological principles identified in chapter 2. It is striking how pieces of the biblical tradition, especially the Old Testament, seem to speak specifically to the issues addressed in this book. This chapter will also note some New Testament references, some of which harken back to the Old Testament. In addition, this chapter will explore some recent social/theological statements produced by various Christian denominations, such as the ELCA's declarations on care of creation, economic justice, and genetics and Pope Francis's encyclical *Laudato si'*.

Chapter 4 will delve into the art of Christian leadership in a hungry world. For all my years of pastoring, mentoring interns and new pastors, and teaching, I have stood on the principle that leadership is an art, not a science. How one integrates the sociology of the community, the secular (sometimes harsh) realities of economics and public policy, and the powerful presence of God and God's word is vital for faithful leadership. It is in that nexus that God's mission can gain traction. It is in those moments that people who disagree politically can sometimes find common ground around the seminal reality that everyone must eat. That reality is not a right; it is not a privilege; it just is. But leading communities to engage in that conversation is an art of socioeconomic-theological integration. In this chapter, we will reflect on how the world's story (chapter 1), the community's story (chapter 2), and God's story (chapter 3) are woven into a shared story—*our* story. The world is hungry in many ways, not the least of which are hunger for faithful truth and the physical reality that more and more people need to eat amid social systems that are often unjust, where some have much and some go without.

Finally, in chapter 5, I will explore some of the potential future realities of food and sustainability issues without pretending to be prophetic. It is not that difficult, if one is attentive, to discern where certain trends are heading. The United States' *Fourth National Climate Assessment* issued in November 2018 and regular reports of the United Nations Framework Convention on Climate Change make some shocking projections related to food and sustainability. I will also address issues of water quality, access, and ownership—emerging front-burner concerns for international nongovernmental organizations (NGOs) and rural sociologists. We often think of food production as a matter of seed and soil. But you can't have food without water. Global climate change is accelerating water-related concerns, impacting precipitation patterns, sea level change, and the amount of water available for agriculture. Finally, I will ask, How will we continue to bring faithful leadership to the issues of chapter 1 that will evolve into the future? What are those issues, and how do we respond faithfully to a world that is growing ever hungrier?

In the process of writing this book, I reached a point where I struggled to find hope. I frequently felt overwhelmed by the complexity of the rapidly evolving challenges I was attempting to describe. To take it all in is like trying to drink from a fire hose. How can anyone make a difference in the face of the tsunami of global food injustice and climate change? Then I realized that to finish the book, I needed to discover hope. It is said, "Where there is a will, there is a way." There is a will, God's will, and there are ways by which the fire hose can become a garden hose that nurtures the seeds of God's purpose for the creation and God's people. The popular phrase adorning coffee mugs, posters, and protest signs these days creatively expresses the call to determined hope and, appropriately, to the focus of this book: "They tried to bury us, but they didn't know we were seeds." Or as Jesus puts it, "For truly I tell you, if you have faith the size of a mustard seed . . . nothing will be impossible for you" (Matt 17:20).

My mother-in-law, who is now deep into the twilight years of her life, taught me a simple, sweet life lesson. I have come to recognize it as a lesson of hope: there is enough, and everyone gets to eat. She wasn't much of a conversationalist, but she was amazing at hospitality. If someone showed up unexpectedly, she would find a way to squeeze another chair around the family table and extend the soup, or stew, or salad so there was enough for everyone. She wasn't good at telling a story, but she was good at getting someone else to tell one. And, oh, the stories that were told around that table. We broke bread with people from all over the world. I can't name all the languages I heard spoken over a meal. Those experiences of food and fellowship opened my eyes, and the eyes of my children, to a bigger world and bigger challenges. In the intervening years, I have shared many meals with many people in many places. I have eaten things—some that I do not wish to describe—with people I've come to know and love from all around the globe. We told stories and we ate, because everyone must eat.

1

The Lay of the Land

Current Realities

The Rural Church Network met at the offices of the US Department of Agriculture (USDA) in Washington, DC, in the early 2000s, during the first term of then president George W. Bush. We experienced a rather heady couple of days interacting with numerous USDA officials. Even the Secretary of Agriculture, Ann Veneman, met with our group and did a presentation. But the conversation I remember most was with the ranking Democrat on the House Agriculture Committee—Congressman Charles "Charlie" Stenholm of Texas. Charlie was a close acquaintance of one of our leaders and agreed to meet with us in a conference room at the USDA with no aides, no press—just him and us. He was open, unguarded, and delightfully engaging. He spoke for a bit but then asked, "What do you want to know?"—a great question for a leader to ask.

At that moment, Microsoft was being sued by the US government in an antitrust case for bundling software on personal computers. At the same time, Cargill, a privately held US company, was in the process of buying Continental Grain Company (CGC), which originated in Belgium. That purchase would give Cargill majority control of food grains in the United States. No antitrust legislation was being proposed in the United States against the CGC deal. Many of us in that room were paying attention to food production issues, though, and we were aware of the deal. So I asked, "Congressman, you are aware of the Microsoft antitrust suit?" He said, "Yes." And then I asked, "Are you aware of the CGC deal?" He said, "Yes, that has come before the AG Committee." I had my laptop in front of me. I said, "I love this computer. It helps me do what I need to do. But I can't eat it. Isn't food more important, and why isn't the US government questioning one company's control of food?" Congressman Stenholm asked me, "Do you want an honest answer?" Of course, I said I did. He responded, "If we apply the antitrust laws of the US against these companies, they would consummate the deal anyway in Brazil." He implied that some food processing companies are transnational, so national laws are not necessarily binding on them. He also said, "There is no political will to fight these companies because we have a relatively safe and cheap food supply." I asked another question: "Congressman, did I just hear you say our laws are impotent with these companies?" He responded with another, "Do you want an honest answer?" Of course, I did. And he said, "That is what I am saying."

I share this story to underscore the pervasive power of transnational corporations and public policy. This high-level governmental decision made about an economic transaction with international implications seemed disconnected from the lives of the people I served. But this one deal had considerable direct consequences for them in terms of the prices they would receive for their crops and the price of food for everyone who must eat. The influence of transnational corporations and the impact of public policy are a couple of the major issues related to food and sustainability that we will look at in this chapter. What the most significant current issues related to food and sustainability are and how they affect our lives is the basis of this chapter.

Definitions

Before we explore some of those specific issues concerning food and sustainability, we should define some key terms that pertain to the topic. First, let us explore how we define or differentiate the various community contexts in which these issues play out.

How the Census Bureau Defines Rural

To begin, we should establish what is meant by *rural* when used to describe a place or community. Most, but not all, food is produced in rural settings. Basically, there are three ways to define *rural*—by census (population), by culture, and by economics. Since the 1910 US census, *urban* has been defined as any incorporated area with a minimum population of 2,500. Any geography that did not meet that population threshold was by default considered rural. This definition has been carried over for the sake of longitudinal comparison. These numeric definitions can be problematic. The urban threshold seems quite low. Many urban people scoff at the idea that an area with a population of only 2,500 would be considered urban. And though *rural* is understood as any area without an incorporated place of at least 2,500 people, census data from 2010 reveal that is still significant in terms of the amount of land and number of people. "Rural areas cover 97 percent of the nation's land area but contain 19.3 percent of the population (about 60 million people)," Census Bureau Director John H. Thompson said.[1] It should be noted that until the 1920 census, more people lived in rural settings than in urban settings in the United States. It was not until 2007 that the global population switched from majority rural to majority urban. Since 1920, a minority of our population is living in US rural settings, and a subset of them is raising food, which everyone needs, while tending to a large percentage of the land. At the same time, more than 80 percent of our population, all consumers of food, are living in the 3 percent urban landmass. The small numeric census threshold for rural areas does not reflect the substantial importance of the land considering the vast size of the geography and its role in producing food.

Let us look at how a metropolitan area is defined. This is a definition that the US Census Bureau has been refining over recent decades. Beginning with *urban* defined as any incorporated area with a minimum population of 2,500, *urban clusters* are defined as urban areas containing at least 2,500 and less than 50,000 people. The US Office of Management and Budget (OMB), for the sake of statistical analysis and government resource allocation, further refines these definitions. According to the OMB, a *metropolitan statistical area* is an urban area of 50,000 or more people, which can include suburbs and even whole counties. The OMB also designates *micropolitan statistical areas*, a term that refers to urban clusters of more than 10,000 but less than 50,000 people. These metropolitan and micropolitan areas can even cross state lines. Counties that contain these statistical zones are often referred to as metropolitan or micropolitan counties. Those that do not are usually referred to as nonmetropolitan counties.

Though the Census Bureau and the OMB do not fine-tune the definition of *rural*, people who live in that context do. The people of rural places distinguish between small-town and rural areas, between town and country. Places that have a cluster of population, no matter how small, and a name are considered towns. The people living in the countryside, around even tiny clusters of population, are considered rural or country people. The first community I lived in as an ordained minister had a population of 100. As someone who had come from a metropolitan statistical area, I thought of the community as rural. They thought of themselves as a town. There was another community two miles away that had a name and a population of 26 people. That was considered a separate town as well. Those of my parishioners who farmed the land around these communities were thought of as rural. The distinction matters to those who live in those settings. It is an acknowledgment that the lifestyles and, often, the vocations of those in the country are different from those in town. But the demarcation between what is town and what is rural is still a bit fuzzy. When I was ordained in the late 1980s, my denomination— the Evangelical Lutheran Church in America (ELCA)—sought to respect this distinction and defined *small town* as a community of 5,000 or less that was not open-country rural, which meant the congregations and the parsonage were not located in a town. But now the ELCA benchmark for a small town is 10,000 or less, which fits nicely with the census definition that *urban* means 2,500 or more and *micropolitan* means more than 10,000 but less than 50,000. It has become a laugh line in presentations I do for small-town and rural church leaders when I note that a respected rural sociologist now defines *small town* as a community of 25,000 or less. They look at a community of upward of 20,000 as "the city," where they go to shop at large discount department stores and large grocery stores, dine in multiple restaurants, and perhaps enjoy a mall and a multiplex cinema. In summary, statistical definitions of community settings are helpful for certain purposes, such as the analysis of population change, but such definitions do not adequately reflect rural people's understanding of their place. But there are other ways of defining *rural*.

Cultural and Economic Definitions of Rural

Perhaps a better way to define *small town* and *rural* is either culturally or economically or both. The *Encyclopedia Britannica Online* defines a rural society as one in which "there is a low ratio of inhabitants to open land and in which the most important economic activities are the production of foodstuffs, fibres, and raw materials."[2] This definition points to an understanding that rural society, or rural culture, is shaped by socioeconomics related to the land. Dr. John Baldwin, a professor of intercultural communication at Illinois State University, describes *rural* as both cultural and economic: "An overview of the rural culture would be a culture that is smaller and more self-dependent. Rural cultures are often based upon a large business in a small area. In a lot of cases, farming is the main industry in a rural area. These types of areas are less populated and more spread out, covering a great amount of land. Houses may have larger yards and rivers, lakes, and ponds are plentiful. The people in rural areas generally live a slower lifestyle and feel a strong bond to their community."[3]

Commonly, five natural resource extraction industries are recognized by economists and sociologists. They are farming, ranching/herding, fishing, mining, and timbering. I would add a sixth, recreation. Many tourist and retirement destinations are located in small-town and rural contexts where the natural beauty of a place is the primary draw. A rural community is often engaged in the production of food, fiber, and fuel. Food is obvious. Fiber refers to the nonsynthetic materials used for clothing, paper, building materials, and so on. Fuel is often mining related—oil, natural gas, coal, uranium—but also includes newer renewable energy sources such as solar and wind. Most large-scale solar and wind farms are located in rural and small-town contexts. Three of the six resource extraction industries are food production related. Those places need to tend to environmental sustainability issues as matters of first-order concern. Their livelihoods depend on it.

I would contend that a cultural-economic definition of the small-town and rural context is more helpful than a census-based one. A cultural-economic definition acknowledges that small-town and rural people have a culture that is different from that of people who live in a metropolitan context. The economic side of this definition is more precise in that it reflects the reality that most people in small-town and rural contexts derive their living in relationship to the extraction of natural resources or in support of those who do. How community functions is shaped by this deep relationship to the land. Small-town and rural people think, act, and approach the issues of food and sustainability differently from those who come from more metropolitan settings. This is important to understand for anyone who seeks to bring leadership in ministry in these communities. We will explore those cultural distinctions more in chapter 2. To conclude, there is a cultural-economic relationship between people and place, community and creation in small-town and rural places.

Other Definitions

Another set of terms that pertain to our topic—*environment, ecosystem, land,* and *soil*—should be defined. Obviously, food and sustainability involve, in varying degrees, the interaction of humans with the rest of the natural world. *Environment* tends to be used as a more empirical, neutral, and scientific term. There is an academic discipline of environmental science, and hence there are environmental scientists. When there is debate about global climate change, the question becomes, "How does this affect our environment?" The word *ecosystem* is frequently used, sometimes synonymously, with *environment.* It is a term, according to *Merriam-Webster,* that refers to "the complex of a community of organisms and its environment functioning as an ecological unit."[4] So *ecosystem* implies some communal relationship with the environment— a community of living things in an interconnected relationship.

And now onto *land*. When I use the term *the land*, I am referring to more than a place or a piece of ground. I am referring to the flora and fauna, both wild and domesticated; the soil; the water; and the air. *The land* carries some biblical weight, especially in the Old Testament tradition: "I will bring you into *the land* that I swore to give to Abraham, Isaac, and Jacob; I will give it to you for a possession. I am the Lord" (Exod 6:8). That reference to land is about a particular geography, though weighted with theological significance—the Promised Land, the Holy Land. But a lot of the Hebrew Scriptures, or the Old Testament, wrap this concept of the land with codes and laws that transcend a particular place. Some of these codes and laws are based on an amazingly broad understanding of the land that seems to speak to concern for all of creation, but at the same time, some of these biblical texts are astoundingly particular, speaking to the foci of this book, food and sustainability. Those biblical connections will be a primary focus of chapter 3. Suffice it to say for now, when I use *the land*, I am seeking to capture the connotations of *ecosystem* with biblical-theological implications.

A last clarifying definition would be *soil*. I have learned from the farmers who have befriended and taught me, as well as soil scientists and botanists, that soil is not dirt. Dirt is the stuff that gets in your house or car that makes it messy and needs to be cleaned up. Soil is actually a living thing—composed of organic matter and microorganisms—that supports a highly diverse, interactive community of plants and creatures, including human beings. An excellent documentary, narrated by the actress Jamie Lee Curtis, is called *Dirt! The Movie*. I highly recommend it, though I have qualms with the title. For those who live on and work the land, the distinction between dirt and soil is important. One early spring, a farmer I was visiting knelt in one of his fields just before planting and scooped up a double handful of soil and sniffed it. He said, "The soil is waking up. And remember, Pastor, this is soil; it isn't dirt." Over time, I've learned to recognize that distinct smell of waking soil in the spring. Hence, when I speak of that which provides food, I will talk about soil, not dirt. I encourage you to do the same.

The words we choose to describe people and community, whether from a statistical or cultural perspective, are important. Likewise, the words we choose to describe a place, even the land itself—be that from the perspective of economics or ecosystems— are equally significant. They are important because they communicate our understanding and our attitudes about a people and a place. When we discuss the issues of food, sustainability, and ministry, we should choose our words with thoughtful intention.

Globalization and Consolidation

Now let us explore some of the most significant issues concerning food and sustainability. The congressperson in the opening story of this chapter named some of the significant issues of food and sustainability—the concentration, monopolization, and globalization of the food system. In other words, a few large transnational corporations have market control over a variety of basic food commodities, such as corn and soybeans. This control is particularly evident regarding processed meats: beef, pork, and poultry. Dr. William Heffernan, a rural sociologist at the University of Missouri, Columbia, and a couple of his research assistants tracked this process of consolidation and monopolization over more than a decade and produced a report of their findings for the National Farmers Union in 1999. Their research continued into the mid-2000s. What they found was that in a majority of essential food commodities, four or fewer corporations controlled more than 40 percent of that commodity market, which by a generally agreed-upon economic principle means, in Heffernan's words, "that market was no longer competitive." In stronger terms, it was monopolized. Economically, this is perhaps the biggest issue.[5] A monopolized food system will allow a small number of corporations to influence the cost of food. To maximize profits, these companies will seek to minimize what they pay farmers for their raw products and maximize the price consumers pay for the finished product.

Vertical Integration

Heffernan and his team discovered that national and global food processing companies were working toward vertical integration, or a controlling interest in a particular food commodity from production to wholesale marketing of the processed product. The colloquial descriptions are "from pen to pan" for meat production and "from seed to shelf" in grain production.

Vertical integration involves, for example, the processing company contracting with producers to provide poultry or pork raised in prescribed buildings (often called confinement buildings), or sometimes beef raised in large feedlot operations with prescribed rations, genetics, and finishing weights delivered on a prescribed date in prescribed numbers. Technically, under these contracts, the farmer/producer owns the buildings, the land, and the livestock. But despite taking a bulk of the capital risk at the initial production phase, they do not control the way they produce the food. The trade-off is that if they can fulfill the terms of the contract, they have a guaranteed price locked in and avoid the vagaries of timing a fluctuating open market. Of course, there are penalties for falling short, especially in terms of weight, quality, number, and timing. But when a chicken, a turkey, a hog, or a cow is ready for market, the farmer/producer needs to sell them. Feeding them more than required by the contract translates to financial loss for the producer.

Most of these processing companies work through industrial factory–style processing plants, blending human labor with mechanical technology. In many of these plants, the section where the bird or animal carcass is broken down to salable cuts of meat by humans and machines is called the "fabrication floor"— terminology borrowed from industrial factories. To make this system run efficiently, the processing company needs a dependable supply of birds and animals of relatively uniform size, quality, and number.

Seed companies, which are also chemical companies, are applying much the same principle. A 2013 article from the *Guardian* notes that "over 53% of the world's commercial seed market is controlled by just three firms—Monsanto, DuPont and Syngenta."[6] Since that article was published, German-based Bayer purchased US-based Monsanto. This makes Bayer one of the top three players in the world commercial seed market. But these companies also have controlling interests in herbicides, pesticides, and fertilizers as well as transportation. By controlling a food commodity from "seed to shelf" or "pen to pan," vertical integration is one way these multinational corporations establish market control in the food industry.

Horizontal Integration

Another way market control is established by large multinational companies is by horizontal integration. Through the first third of the twentieth century, food production on the producers' level tended to be quite diverse. A local farmer may have grown a rotation of four or more grains and raised some combination of beef, dairy, poultry, or hogs. An advantage of diversification is resiliency in times of market volatility. For example, if the price of beef is down, there is a strong chance the price of pork is up. Around the time of World War II, farmers were being encouraged, particularly by agricultural schools at land grant universities and the university extension service, to specialize for the sake of efficiency. The basic concept was that farmers were expected to learn to produce one or two commodities—using equipment developed through technological advancement—and supply the food system. At the same time, food processors were diversifying. Several of the top four companies in beef processing are also in the top four in pork processing or poultry processing and even grain processing. For example, companies such as Tyson, Cargill, JBS (Swift), and WH Group (Smithfield) are in the top four of numerous agricultural markets, including

meat and grain products. This is known as horizontal integration, or having controlling market share across a wide variety of
food commodities. Beef and pork producers contribute funds to
the National Cattlemen's Board and the National Pork Board,
respectively, for the promotion of their products. Hence the
slogan "Beef. It's What's for Dinner" or the new slogan for pork,
"Pork: Be Inspired." When Oprah made some public comments
about the safety of beef related to "mad cow disease," discussed
in more detail later in this chapter, beef producers lost sales,
and pork producers benefitted.[7] But the major meat processors
didn't care whether we bought a steak or a pork chop because
they have major interests in both commodities.

The work of Heffernan and his associates has been expanded
and brought into the twenty-first century by Dr. Philip H. Howard, an associate professor in the Department of Community
Sustainability at Michigan State University and a member of the
International Panel of Experts on Sustainable Food Systems. His
research findings are shared in the book *Concentration and Power
in the Food System: Who Controls What We Eat?*[8] This is the most
current and comprehensive treatment of this topic. Having both
sociological and environmental training regarding food production, he brings unique insight into the ethical implications of the
issues involved. His final chapter is titled "Endgame?" In it, he
looks forward, speaking of duopolies rather than monopolies.
He predicts that in the future, two major companies will control
the food system in various commodities, some of which will be
horizontally integrated across commodities. But he ends on a
cautiously hopeful note:

The trend toward greater levels of concentration appears to be unabated, but there are signs that it may eventually fall victim to its own success. Due to the extreme complexity of food systems, it is nearly impossible to predict which negative feedback is likely to play the greatest role in this reversal. . . . Counter-movements play a key role in demonstrating alternative possibilities of food provisioning, preserving seed and livestock diversity, and maintaining the skills and knowledge that will be needed to replace the current system. Joining these movements and supporting the alternatives created by others could therefore be essential to maintaining our ability to feed ourselves in the future.[9]

What Howard is saying is that the larger global food system, in part because of its complexity and in part because monopolistic systems are hard to sustain, will eventually fail. Thus, alternative food systems, what he calls countermovements, will be needed. These countermovements may include such things as more diversified farms, more sustainable farming practices, and localized farm-to-market food systems. He argues that in the meantime, we must nurture those alternatives and preserve the knowledge of how to do them for the sake of sustainability.

Landownership and Control

There are 2.27 billion acres of land in the United States. Seventy-two percent of that land, or about 1.94 billion acres, is privately owned. And obviously, since 97 percent of the US landmass is nonurban, a majority of the privately owned land is in town and country contexts, where the production of food, fiber, and fuel happens. Of that, over 25 million acres (1.3 percent) are owned by just thirty families or individuals. One is a Canadian family. A number of those families either are western ranchers or run timber companies, for which it makes sense to have large holdings to produce food and fiber. It takes a lot of acres per animal to feed beef cattle on the semiarid high plains of North America, and it takes a lot of acres to produce the timber to supply our paper and building material consumption. But many of the largest landowners are billionaires who are using land as a tangible asset to diversify their investment portfolios. Their decisions about how that land is managed are driven by profit motives. Frequently, those decisions do not consider what is best for the local community and, at times, are in direct conflict with the interests of local people. Among these landowners are several who made their fortunes in industries unrelated to food production. They include the cofounder of the Subway sandwich franchise, the cofounder of Teledyne Technologies, and the CEO of Amazon, Jeff Bezos. The two largest landowners are media moguls: CNN founder Ted Turner with 2 million acres, and John Malone, chairperson of Liberty Global Inc., a global media organization, with 2.2 million acres.[10] These are the more extreme examples. But overall, farms and ranches are getting exponentially larger. The landmass is finite, and thus larger holdings mean fewer farming and ranching families, fewer people living on the land, and shrinking rural and small-town communities.

There is nothing illegal in this. But this level of consolidation may have ethical implications concerning neighboring communities and even the sustainability of the land. To Turner's credit, he is using much of his ranch holdings to raise bison meat in an eco-friendly way. Bison, which evolved on the Great Plains, interact with the land differently and have fewer adverse impacts on the environment than cattle. At the same time, he has the largest bison herd on the planet, a personal monopoly of a food commodity. Many of these investment landholders do not live on the land they own. Some have never seen it in person or met any of the people who make up the local community. They seek to optimize the land's financial value; they do not need to drink the water that comes from it nor breathe the air that wafts over it. The local population does. In the Upper Midwest, I witnessed what happened to some large tracts of land bought up by absentee landowners. In one case, extensive soil conservation practices, like grass waterways and hillside terracing installed to prevent erosion and protect surface water quality, were ripped out to put more acres into production. In another case, large hog confinement barns were installed, creating significant air-quality problems for neighboring farmers. The owner did not even live in the state and so was not personally affected. In still another case, an out-state land speculator bought large acreages from retiring farmers at auction well above average land values, tore out windbreaks installed to protect against wind erosion, and significantly raised the rent for that land. Thus outside land speculators can drive up land values, land rental costs, and often property taxes as well as set back local efforts to improve soil and water quality. These consequences are in conflict with the best interests of local people who are seeking to make a living from the land.

The Safety, Availability, and Affordability of Food

Also on the menu of important issues related to food and sustainability are the safety, availability, and affordability of food. At least from the time of Upton Sinclair's novel *The Jungle* (1906), the public has been aware of issues related to food safety. Sinclair intended to shine a light on the immigrant workers employed in the food industry, which I will highlight later in this chapter. The primary impact of the book, however, was to stir concerns about the meat that was being processed and marketed by a growing industrialized food processing system. Simply put, fewer people were eating meat produced by a local farmer—whom you might know, who sent animals to a local butcher, whom you would know—switching to eating meat processed in large operations that were not well inspected for health and safety.

John Steinbeck's novel *Cannery Row* (1945) told a similar story about the Pacific coast fishing industry—focused on the people but raising questions about the safety of our seafood. The issue has not gone away, nor should it. In *Anxious Appetites: Food and Consumer Culture*, Peter Jackson, a professor of human geography at the University of Sheffield, speaks to these issues from a contemporary perspective and identifies numerous food health and safety concerns from scientific, ethical, and psychological perspectives. Jackson asserts, "It is equally important to understand the 'routes' and interconnections through which consumers make sense of where their food comes from and how it is produced. While consumers may be only dimly aware of the globalized nature of contemporary food production or the extent to which power over its production is corporately controlled, anxieties may be provoked by the chronic lack of transparency of such systems."[11] In essence, the disconnect between consumers' understanding about where and how their food is produced not only adds to anxiety over the safety of their food but also necessitates the abdication of the oversight over the safety of their food to governmental agencies and food corporations. This harkens back to something I noted in the introduction from Dr. Christopher J. H. Wright: "We depend on the efficient use of well-maintained farmland to keep us fed and clothed *while we go about our creation and consumption of wealth in other ways many steps removed from direct contact with the land*."[12]

An example of the lack of awareness of how our food is produced and how that affects our food's safety emerged in the late 1990s, when "mad cow disease"—bovine spongiform encephalopathy (BSE)—hit public media awareness. It was first identified in the United Kingdom and was caused by feeding beef cattle ground-up meat scraps and bones from sheep and other cattle as a cheap protein supplement. Cattle are natural herbivores—not carnivores, not even omnivores. Feeding meat protein to herbivores turned into a fatal problem for beef cattle. And BSE has the potential, though rare, of being communicated to humans when they consume beef from an infected animal. In 1996, Oprah Winfrey highlighted this fact on her popular TV program, and beef sales plummeted in the United States. Oprah was subsequently sued by cattlemen in Texas in the US Federal Court of the Northern District of Texas for violation of Texas' False Disparagement of Perishable Food Products Act. The case hinged on free speech rights, and Oprah won.[13] But for the general public, this affair was more about understanding where our food comes from, how it is produced, and whether it is safe.

Other factors contribute to unease over food safety. Debates still circle around the use of synthetic growth hormones in dairy and beef cattle to increase productivity. Milk producers label packaging "non-BGH"—no added bovine growth hormones—as a marketing strategy. And there is continued discussion in the medical community about the human health impacts of using antibiotics prophylactically in large confinement poultry and pork producing facilities. These drugs are used to prevent loss of flocks or herds in tight quarters to disease and increase the rate of weight gain. The concern is that this application of drugs, such as Cipro, might be diminishing the effectiveness of those antibiotics for human use by creating bacterial resistance. In addition, the United States has experienced a growing number of food recalls, which increases concern among consumers over food safety. A recent study by the USDA's Economic Research Service revealed that "the number of food product recalls has increased significantly over the past couple of decades. . . . While the number of food product recalls increased across every food category, the increase was statistically significant only for grain products, animal products, and prepared foods and meals."[14] Each of these high-profile, large-scale recalls along with the unresolved questions concerning the long-term effects of growth hormones and prophylactic antibiotics heighten the public's anxiety regarding food safety.

But the availability and affordability of food is a significant issue as well. Unfortunately, though the United States produces an abundance of healthy food, and much of it gets exported to other countries, that food is not accessible to many places in the country. These places have been termed *food deserts*, which the USDA defines

> as low-income tracts in which a substantial number or proportion of the population has low access to supermar-kets or large grocery stores. Low-income tracts are char-acterized by either a poverty rate equal to or greater than 20 percent, or a median family income that is 80 percent or less of the metropolitan area's median family income (for tracts in metropolitan areas) or the statewide median family income (for tracts in nonmetropolitan areas). Low access is characterized by at least 500 people and/ or 33 percent of the tract population residing more than 1 mile from a supermarket or large grocery in urban areas, and more than 10 miles in rural areas.[15]

USDA researchers also note, "Some low-income communities in the United States lack stores that sell healthy and affordable food. The lack of store access in these communities—sometimes called food deserts—may contribute to poor diet, obesity, and other diet-related illness."[16] Notably, obesity is a major contributor to numerous other health issues, including diabetes. A report of the Centers for Disease Control and Prevention (CDC) issued in

2017 shows that over one hundred million Americans are living with diabetes or prediabetes.[17]

Food availability is related to affordability. Even in places where whole foods are available, many people cannot afford them, because whole foods are significantly more expensive than highly processed, prepackaged foods. In the documentary movie *Food, Inc.*, this issue is addressed in a segment called "The Dollar Menu." It features a lower-middle-income Latino American family of four and their struggles to make decisions about how best to use the money they have available for food. The mother, Mrs. Gonzalez, says, "We didn't even think about eating healthy because we thought everything is healthy. Now that I know that the food is really unhealthy for us, I feel guilty giving it to our kids. When you have only a dollar to spend, and you have two kids to feed, either you go to the market and try to find something that's cheap or just straight to a drive-through and get two small hamburgers. . . . This is what will fill her up, not that one single item at the market."[18]

To check this, I did some research of my own. Financially, I have been privileged. Most of the time, I purchase food without considering the cost. I may choose what is in season, which is often the cheaper option, but cost is not my primary concern. I went to a local grocery in a community near where I live in small-town and rural Iowa. First, the selection of fresh produce was quite limited. A bunch of broccoli costs $2.69. Bell peppers were two for $1.00. Apples were $1.29 per pound (two apples). A head of iceberg lettuce, not the most nutritious of the lettuce options, was $1.29. Small bags of precut mixed lettuce were $3.29. In the meat department, the cheapest of the ground beef was $1.99 per pound. When I perused the frozen meal section, I found a variety of processed, prepackaged meals for between $1.29 and $1.49. Of course, they are mass-produced with inferior ingredients and preservatives, but they cost less than a bunch of broccoli. At the nearest fast-food chain, I could buy two cheese burgers for $2.00. I could get the meal option, which includes a medium fry and a medium drink, for less than $5.00. Those for whom financial realities are particularly challenging are often forced to choose between eating healthy and eating what is most affordable.

This is a global issue. According to numerous respected international food organizations, such as the United Nations' Food and Agriculture Organization (FAO) and Oxfam, enough food is produced globally each year to feed 10 billion people. The current estimated population of the planet is 7.6 billion. In an article for HuffPost, Eric Holt-Giménez, director of the Institute for Food and Development Policy, asserts, "Hunger is caused by poverty and inequality, not scarcity. For the past two decades, the rate of global food production has increased faster than the rate of global population growth. The world already produces more than 1½ times enough food to feed everyone on the planet. That's enough to feed 10 billion people, the population peak we expect by 2050. But the people making less than $2 a day—most of whom are resource-poor farmers cultivating unviably small plots of land—can't afford to buy this food."[19]

I witnessed the reality of the impact of poverty on nutrition in my work in the villages of KwaZulu-Natal, South Africa. We were invited by our Zulu Christian brothers and sisters to partner with them in establishing community gardens to grow nutritional food locally. They had land that had been given back to them after apartheid ended, but they needed training and equipment to make it productive. Most of our dedicated, faithful partners could not afford to buy fresh food in the white Afrikaner grocery stores, which were not located in the villages anyway. A high percentage of the Zulu villagers were overweight, and many lived with diabetes. In addition, South Africa is often referred to as the "epicenter of the HIV-AIDS pandemic."[20] The drugs used to fight the disease are far less effective when nutrition is low. They require a good diet, which is not readily available or affordable.

The safety, affordability, and availability of food are complex issues that challenge those who produce food and those who need to eat. These are issues of national and global concern.

Environmental Sustainability

How food is grown significantly affects the health and sustainability of our environment. I have learned from my years living in a prairie ecosystem that diversity is resilience. If you toss a Hula-Hoop (roughly three feet in diameter) on a natural or restored prairie, within that hoop are hundreds of species. Prairie plants and flowers, insects, birds, small and large mammals, and microorganisms within the soil help build soil fertility and health. Some species thrive in high rain periods, some in drought conditions, and thus a prairie is naturally sustainable. A prairie is a polyculture of perennial species. Modern agriculture seeks to take diversity out of the system and make a piece of land grow only one thing annually, be it corn, soybeans, wheat, or some other crop. A farm field is a monoculture of annual species, counter to what makes an ecosystem most fertile.

To create this monoculture, nonnatural inputs—herbicides, pesticides, and fertilizers—are often required. Those inputs affect not just the farm field but the larger natural environment, including water quality. We see these cascading effects in the hypoxia zone, or "dead zone," in the Gulf of Mexico—the result of nutrients (nitrogen and phosphorus, primarily) running from fields into the Mississippi River and its tributaries, which empty into the Gulf. Those nutrients create algae blooms, which use up the oxygen in the water that fish and other species need to survive. The National Oceanic and Atmospheric Administration (NOAA) measures this phenomenon annually. In 2017, the dead zone in the Gulf was the largest ever recorded, covering 8,776 square miles—roughly the size of the state of New Jersey.[21] Not only does this dead zone impact the natural aesthetics of the coast line; it affects fisheries and those who provide us seafood as well.[22]

Much of this nutrient runoff is from agricultural sources, but not all. Urban dwellers contribute as well with fertilizers applied to lawns, parks, and golf courses, often in excessive amounts. Because most farmers are operating under slim profit margins, many use modern technology, like computer-controlled, GPS-guided application equipment, to apply fertilizer at just the right points and in just the right amount to minimize costs and waste. Nonetheless, how food is raised can have significant, long-lasting, and often unintended consequences for all of the creation.

There are other, subtler impacts. Overspray and wind drift from pesticides and herbicides harm beneficial species of insects, especially pollinators, and plants. The elimination of fencerows and windbreaks to make it easier to use larger tractors and combines also destroys natural habitat for numerous species of native plants. One example is milkweed, which is essential for monarch butterflies, an important pollinator, and the populations of both milkweed and monarchs are in decline. Populations of bees, perhaps the key pollinator, are diminishing at alarming rates. The loss of insects, plants, and other living things isn't a new phenomenon, however. Rachel Carson, biologist and environmental activist, wrote a seminal book, *Silent Spring*, in 1962. The premise of the book, based on the science of the time, was that pesticides, particularly dichloro-diphenyl-trichloroethane (DDT), were permeating the environment as they worked their way through the natural food chain, and one indicator of that was the loss of birds. As she poetically articulates,

> For each of us, as for the robin in Michigan or the Salmon in the Miramichi, this is a problem of ecology, of inter-relationships, of interdependence. . . . We poison the gnats in a lake and the poison travels from link to link of the food chain and soon the birds of the lake margins become its victims. We spray our elms and the following *springs are silent of robin song*, not because we sprayed the robins directly but because the poison traveled, step by step, through the now familiar elm leaf-earthworm-robin cycle. These are matters of record, observable, part of the visible world around us. They reflect the web of life—or death—that scientists know as ecology.[23]

Carson's book and her subsequent defense of its premise are considered by many to be the triggers of the modern environmental movement. Chemical companies pushed back hard. But eventually, DDT was banned, and the movement that grew out of Carson's work resulted in the establishment of the US Environmental Protection Agency (EPA). (Carson received the Presidential Medal of Freedom posthumously from President Jimmy Carter.)

Wendell Berry is a novelist, poet, philosopher, environmental activist, and farmer. He uses the fencerow, vegetation left in its natural state surrounding a farm field, to underscore the ongoing creative importance of diversity and the need for the natural creation to interact with the domesticated creation. If that creative diversity is eliminated, then the potential for regenerative sustainability is diminished or perhaps lost. He says, "If change is to come, it will have to come from the outside. It will have to come from the margins."[24]

At this point, I need to address global climate change as an issue. I confess my personal and pastoral frustration that this is a matter of debate—that some people argue that climate change is not real. Well over 90 percent of reputable scientists globally say it is occurring and back up the claim with data. Perhaps there is room for debate about causality—human, natural, or some combination thereof—but it seems clear that change is upon us. And that change will affect food production: what, where, and when it can be produced. It is already affecting ranching, farming, and fisheries. Will the wheat farming and ranching areas of the semi-arid Great Plains of North America become a desert? Will the fertile, row-cropped prairies of North America become semiarid plains? What will happen to the aquifers and the availability of water? What will happen to the fisheries as ocean levels rise and temperatures and currents change? Similar questions are being asked about ecosystems around the world. I do not pretend that I have any expertise in this matter, but I know it is important, because everyone must eat.

Genetics

Another major issue related to food and sustainability is the genetic altering of seed, plants, and livestock. Genetic engineering of food using genetically modified organisms (GMOs) has been a topic of debate for several decades. Genetic manipulation (GM) had its first practical applications in agriculture. Of course, gene sequencing and gene therapies are being applied to humans now with the hope of developing cures for or perhaps eradicating certain diseases or conditions. Actually, farmers have been doing forms of genetic manipulation for millennia, selecting wild plants and animals for certain characteristics and cross-pollinating and crossbreeding to replicate and enhance those important qualities for food or fiber. Essentially, the farmer intervened in the natural processes of botany and animal biology to improve genetics. So a farmer would observe the cornfield and save the cobs (seed) from the best plants and use that seed to replant next season. As that process repeated, the farmer developed a corn variety specially adapted to his or her microecosystem. Likewise, a hog farmer would observe the sows in the herd and the piglets they produced and the boar that sired them. The highest-quality animals would become part of the breeding stock, and the rest would go to market. Sometimes the farmer would introduce genetics from another breed to incorporate or enhance certain qualities in the herd. This process has been used in all livestock production.

What is different now, with the advancement of science and technology, is that rudimentary farm-level genetics is being supplemented by transgenics—the technology and industry of splicing genes into plants and animals to create the desired qualities. Sometimes that involves implanting a gene from a different species of a different biological order, such as implanting an animal gene into a plant. The first example of a transgenic whole food product intended for the grocery store was the Flavr Savr tomato developed by Calgene, which is owned by Monsanto. Calgene spliced genetic material from *E. coli* bacteria, which comes from the digestive tracts of mammals, into the tomato DNA, forming recombinant DNA to produce a more resilient tomato with a longer shelf life. In other words, the tomato didn't bruise or rot as quickly as nontransgenic tomatoes. It worked, but the marketing was not successful. Opponents of such biotechnology dubbed it the "Frankentomato" and other such transgenic foods as "Frankenfoods," so it was not commercially viable. Experiments are ongoing to implant genes from cold water salmon and flounder into tomatoes and strawberries to make them more frost resistant to extend the growing season.

But other transgenic plants have been commercially successful. Seedless watermelons are produced by crossing a diploid watermelon, a natural melon with two sets of chromosomes that produce fertile seeds, with a tetraploid watermelon that has been chemically changed to have four sets of chromosomes. The resulting cross-pollination is a hybrid (with three sets of chromosomes) that cannot produce seeds and is very popular with consumers. GM corn and cotton, designated Bt-corn and Bt-cotton, has bacterial genes implanted in the seed that allows the plant to produce its own pesticide. So when corn borers, corn rootworms, corn earworms, or cotton boll weevils attack the plant, the pests die. Monsanto developed Roundup, a broad-spectrum herbicide that kills annual broad-leaf weeds and grasses. Then Monsanto developed GM seeds, called Roundup Ready, for a variety of crops, and those crops are immune to Roundup. That allows the field to be sprayed with Roundup and kill every plant except the crop. In turn, Bayer CropScience has developed a similar product called Liberty, which works on weeds that have become resistant to Roundup, and seed stock called LibertyLink. More such products are yet to come as agricultural biotech companies are continuing to create genetically modified seeds that are coupled with specific herbicides.

And then there is cloning. You may be familiar with Dolly the sheep, the first large mammal successfully cloned, a procedure that took place in Scotland in 1996. Note that Dolly was an agricultural animal. Dolly went on to produce six lambs. She died almost seven years later due to lung disease, which is not uncommon in sheep and was unrelated to her being a clone. Many companies are pursuing animal cloning, and the leader among them is BGI Genomics in southern China. According to an article by the science editor of BBC News, BGI has the world's largest number of gene sequencing machines (156) and operate what they call a cloning factory focusing on hogs. As the company says on its web-site, "Population growth and climate change are creating unique challenges for food supply across the world. BGI offers a wide range of agricultural genomics (agrigenomics) solutions, which are helping to drive both increased food supply and sustainable production. Our agrigenomics technologies are helping plant and animal breeders and researchers identify desirable traits, leading to healthier and more productive crops and livestock."[25] The hogs they are cloning, approximately five hundred each year for now, are intended to promote genetics for increased meat production and medical experimentation. Because genetically, hogs are very close to humans, they are excellent candidates for pharmaceutical and gene therapy experiments for human treatments.

Experimentation is also underway to raise hogs as possible organ donors for transplants from hogs to humans, a process known as xenotransplantation. As of February 2017, Chinese surgeons have performed more than four hundred hog cornea implants into humans with a 95 percent success rate.[26] Arteries and heart valves from hogs and cattle are regularly used for transplan-tation in the United States. Another Chinese corporation, WH Group, which now owns Smithfield, a US-based company that is the largest pork company in the world, is pursuing this biotechnol-ogy branch. A hog's kidneys, lungs, liver, and heart are all similar in size and pulmonary makeup to humans, making it possible for xenotransplantation. As Courtney Stanton, vice president of Smithfield's bioscience unit, said in an interview with Reuters, "Our bread and butter has always been the bacon, sausage, fresh pork—very much a food-focused operation. We want to signal to the medical device and science communities that this is an area we're focused on—that we're not strictly packers."[27] Raising livestock for organ xenotransplant into humans is being made possible by a new technology that is time efficient, relatively affordable, and not that difficult to use. It is called CRISPR—an acronym for clustered regularly interspaced short palindromic repeats. This method allows technicians to strip from hogs viral genes that could lead to transplant rejection in humans. Cloned hogs, genetically modified, could make xenotransplantation viable.

All of this technology has numerous ethical implications. Basically, any seed, plant, or animal that has been genetically modified or cloned is considered a new variety and thus can be patented and claimed as property by the company that modified it. This means that anyone who wants to take advantage of the seed's or the animal's modified genetics has to buy them directly from the company. Agribusinesses aggressively prosecute anyone suspected of violating their patents. Sometimes this so-called violation results from genetic drift. If a patented variety is planted next to a field that is planted with an open-pollinated variety, and the pollen from the former drifts into the latter, cross-pollination can occur. This can lead to lawsuits against the owner of the cross-pollinated field. An article from the *Guardian* notes that "over 53% of the world's commercial seed market is controlled by just three firms—Monsanto, DuPont and Syngenta." In addition, according to a report by the Center for Food Safety, in recent years, "Monsanto had brought against farmers and found some 142 patent infringement suits against 410 farmers and 56 small businesses in more than 27 states. In total the firm has won more than $23m from its targets." Debbie Barker, an expert with the organization Save Our Seeds, is quoted in that same article, saying, "Corporations did not create seeds and many are challenging the existing patent system that allows private companies to assert ownership over a resource that is vital to survival and that historically has been in the public domain."[28] The patenting of seed has global implications as well. Many farmers in the Global North and Global South cannot afford to buy seed every year and are reliant on the old system of saving seed to replant the following year.

Some people question the ethicality and safety of creating transgenetic food crops, cloning animals for human experimentation, and harvesting animal organs for xenotransplantation. The use of Roundup Ready crops and others like them has resulted in significant losses of beneficial native plants such as milkweed. Pollen that drifts from Bt-corn can land on native plants that feed the larvae of beneficial insects like butterflies and can potentially kill them if ingested.[29] Larger seed companies are buying out smaller ones and, in most cases, discontinuing production of their competing seed varieties, decreasing the diversity in the system.

Paul Raeburn, an Associated Press science editor and author of *The Last Harvest: The Genetic Gamble That Threatens to Destroy American Agriculture*, documents an event that took place in 1970 that was devastating to US corn farmers. Hybrid varieties of corn were being developed that were fast growing and high yielding but low in resistance to pathogens. That year, 85 percent of the US corn crop was planted with varieties that shared a common trait—Texas male-sterile cytoplasm, or T cytoplasm. This made the tassels at the top of the plant sterile, which saved time and money to detassel them by hand and allowed the plant to put more energy toward producing cobs and kernels. But a fungus commonly called southern corn leaf blight could infect the genetic material in T cytoplasm, damaging or killing the corn plant. It started in the southeastern United States, devastating crops in the Deep South. Then it worked its way up the central United States to the Corn Belt of the Upper Midwest and eventually into Canada. Over one billion bushels of corn were lost. Corn prices tripled—a boon to corn farmers who hadn't planted the vulnerable hybrids but a bane to livestock farmers who used corn in their feed and to consumers of corn-based processed foods. GM has many benefits, but there are significant potential problems as well.

New Immigrants Working in Food Production and Processing

The issue of immigration is frequently in the news, particularly related to the presence of undocumented immigrants in the United States. Many immigrants, documented and undocumented, work in our food system and are vital to the system's success. This became apparent to me on a snowy winter morning in 1992. I woke up and turned on the local radio station to find out whether my children's school would be delayed or canceled because of the weather. That morning, for the first time, the school announcement for Worthington, Minnesota (with a population of approximately twelve thousand at the time), was given in five languages, one of which was English. I realized something had changed.

What had changed was the pork packing plant, the largest employer in that small city. At one time, working in the packing plant was a difficult but well-paid blue-collar job. In the late 1980s, the workers' unions were broken, the processing lines were sped up, and wages and benefits were reduced. European Americans quit. So the company brought in workers of other cultural backgrounds for whom those jobs were better than what they could find elsewhere. The company began by hiring along the southern border of the United States and bussed recruits to Minnesota. Some were already US citizens. Many were undocumented.

Today, nearly twenty languages are spoken in Worthington, and nearly eighty language variants are spoken in the Worthington school district. Worthington has grown to more than 13,000 in population. The JBS pork processing plant (a Brazilian company) in Worthington employs more than 2,200 people who speak eighteen major languages, including Amharic, Arabic, Dinka, Hmong, Karen, Laotian, Vietnamese, Spanish, French, and English. This sudden influx of people from new immigrant cultures stressed social services, emergency services, and the school system. New policies needed to be developed. Interpreters needed to be identified and trained for the police department, court system, hospital and clinic system, and schools. These changes occurred not only in Worthington proper but also in smaller satellite towns, where many of the new neighbors settled because the housing was less expensive. This new reality has been replicated across the country—anywhere meat is being processed and produce is being grown and picked.

The growing number of new immigrants is frequently received with apprehension. US immigration policy has been hotly debated in recent years. There are calls to keep immigrants out and deport those who are in the country illegally. Attempts to enforce immigration laws have resulted in children being separated from their parents when crossing the southern border and numerous Immigration and Customs Enforcement (ICE) raids on meat processing plants and other businesses. There are also calls to find a path to citizenship for immigrants and to maintain the Deferred Action for Childhood Arrivals (DACA) program in response to legal attempts to eliminate it. This program allows children who meet specific requirements to stay in the United States if they were brought there by parents who were not legally authorized to be in the country. A large number of the immigrants around whom these controversies swirl work at providing our food. According to a *Washington Post* article, "Estimates of the number of farmworkers employed in the United States vary. According to Robert Guenther, senior vice president for public policy for the United Fresh Produce Association, a produce industry trade group, it's about 1.5 million to 2 million. Of those, a large portion is illegal. Again, estimates vary, but Guenther puts it at 50 to 70 percent, a wide range."[30] The Department of Labor's National Agricultural Workers Survey estimates 46 percent. The Department of Labor estimates that more than 77,000 people work in slaughtering and packing meat. These numbers do not include those who work in the restaurant industry.

Padma Lakshmi, a *New York Times* best-selling author, winner of the 2016 Ellis Island Medal of Honor, host of the TV show *Top*

Chef, and an immigrant herself, reflects on the role of immigrant labor in the food industry:

> I think the food landscape in this country would be completely different without immigrant labor. They don't want to cause trouble. They will do the grunt work that nobody else is willing to do, because they have to support themselves, their families, they also often send money back to their birth countries. And so a lot of them are really afraid to speak up. But, everybody has the right to be treated in a dignified manner. Immigrants are people too. We just want to work hard. We just want the same thing for our children that anyone else wants for theirs. We all have a responsibility to reach down and pull up the people who really break their back for you day in and day out.[31]

The notion, asserted by some, that immigrants are taking away jobs from US citizens is just not accurate. Without immigrant labor, the food industry would be crippled, which is why many large food producers and food processors support sensible immigration reform.

Many other issues could have been lifted up in this chapter, but those that have been presented are the major ones in my estimation. A report prepared for the National Farmers Union and read into the congressional record states,

> One often hears the statement that agriculture is changing and we must adapt to the changes. Few persons who repeat the statement really understand the magnitude of

the changes and the implications of them for agriculture and for the long-term sustainability of the food system. It is almost heresy to ask if these changes are what the people of our country really want or, if they are not what is desired, how we might redirect the change. The changes are the result of notoriously short-sighted market forces and not the result of public dialogue, the foundation of a democracy. . . . The centralized food system that continues to emerge was never voted on by the people of this country, or for that matter, the people of the world. It is the product of deliberate decisions made by a very few powerful human actors. This is not the only system that could emerge. Is it not time to ask some critical questions about our food system and about what is in the best interest of this and future generations?[32]

The final question is worth pondering. In various ways, we will grapple with it in subsequent chapters.

Questions for Reflection and Discussion

1. If you were to choose to further explore one of the issues named in this chapter, which one would it be and why?

2. What other issues related to the food system, not named in this chapter, are you aware of that are worth discussing?

3. We are all consumers of food, because everyone must eat. How would you engage in conversation about the issues you named in the first two questions with a farmer or rancher whose vocation is to raise your food within the challenges of the modern food system? What would you say to or ask them?

4. As ministry leaders, how might we join the larger societal conversation Heffernan calls for "to ask some critical questions about our food system and about what is in the best interest of this and future generations?"

5. How does your faith inform these issues for you?

2

People and Place, Land and Community

Sociological Connections

On a dark September day, the clouds hung leaden in the sky, threatening rain and once again thwarting the heat of the sunshine needed to mature the crops. The weather had been this way for most of the spring, summer, and fall of 1993. Rain washed the Upper Midwest in epic proportions, flooding rivers, washing out fields, and devastating the crops. Pastors and people had prayed in earnest for relief. Now most were resigned to the reality that there would be little or no harvest, another economic blow to a region that had struggled for the better part of fifteen years. The government responded as best it could with economic aid, the cornerstone of which was a program called Zero-92, a cash payment based on a percentage of the farmer's crop the previous year. The catch was that the farmer had to destroy whatever crop was in the field, "zero out; plow it under," in order to receive the payment. One would think that the decision would be straightforward. With a crop of literally no monetary value in the field, the promise of some payment made economic sense.

On that dark overcast day, my neighbor stopped to visit Shalom Hill Farm (SHF), where I lived and worked in southwestern Minnesota, and the subject quickly turned to the harvest. He pointed to the field adjacent to our place and said, "For thirty years I have farmed that piece of land and have taken what the Lord has given me—good or bad, mostly good. Now I am supposed to tell the Lord it's not good enough and plow it under and take the government money. Pastor Mark, I just can't do it." For this man, this farmer, the decision was about more than just economics; it involved his relationship to God. He was not alone. I heard numerous simple yet profound faith statements that season. One farmer, as she shared her tension and frustration with the continued rain, said, "We have been farming out here for more than a hundred years, and we've been pretty hard on the land. Maybe God is trying to tell us something. Maybe God is forcing us to give the land a rest." One man, having made the decision to plow under his crop and take the aid payment, made one pass through his field with the plow, got out of his tractor, and vomited. The act of destroying something he had worked so hard to create and care for overwhelmed him and made him physically ill.

Part of me ached for these people. But to be honest, deep down inside, I rejoiced. Here were people who cared. Here were people for whom their vocation was about more than money. Here were people who cared about what God thought, cared about the land, and cared about what it meant to grow food.

For many who live out food sustainability and ministry, there is a deep connection between place and people, creation and community. There is a sense of rootedness to place that is deeply significant, and those of us called to engage in the ministry component of this mixture should pay close attention to this reality. Those who lead need to be careful to not fall into nostalgia for an idyllic and often unrealistic memory of the past. But the failure to tend to the relationship between land and people is a huge miscalculation.

The Rise of Rural Sociology

I discovered early in my ministry that in addition to biblical and theological knowledge, I needed to understand rural sociology. I grew up in a suburban metropolitan context. The three-street, four-block neighborhood of my youth had five times the population of the first town I lived in as a pastor. In my suburban upbringing, my many neighbors lived nearby, but most I did not know. Later, I didn't give a second thought to driving across the city to shop at a particular store for what I wanted. I drove thirty miles to work, and during rush hour, that might have taken forty-five minutes to an hour. When I was a young adult, the people I worked with as a sign painter had nothing in common with my church community or my academic community. It became apparent to me during my first years of ministry that community and communication in the small-town and rural context in which I was serving functioned differently. To be a good servant, I needed to understand the people I was sent to serve. But in my ministry training, sociology—let alone rural sociology—was not a required discipline. To fill in the gaps in my understanding, I joined rural ministry guilds and associations, used my continuing education time with intention, and read.

To my delight, I also discovered I was not alone in this need. Historically, the specific academic discipline of rural sociology has deep roots in the church. In an award-winning paper presented to the Rural Sociological Society, "The Institutional and Intellectual Origins of Rural Sociology," Suzanne Smith, director of the Augustana Research Institute, states, "The representation of rural sociology in seminaries and Bible colleges is notable, showing the discipline's close ties to religious reform and missionary impulses to improve country life and sustain country churches."[1]

The genesis of rural sociology took place in the late 1800s and early 1900s, when vast tracts of rural land in North America were being populated with small communities composed largely of new immigrants. More people lived in a rural context than in an urban one. In addition, food production needed to be done differently in North American ecosystems. To meet that need, US land grant universities were charged with establishing agricultural schools and, later, the county extension service to research and teach techniques for food production on the US prairies and plains. Public policy in the United States, such as the Land Grant Act of 1862 and land grants to railroads, impacted how communities were organized. The act was a remarkably progressive piece of legislation that offered settlers 160 acres that they were required to live on and improve for at least five years. It is important to note that the five-year stipulation coincided with the immigration policy of the time—that is, after declaring one's intention for citizenship and living in the country for five years, one qualified for US citizenship. The land grants to railroads resulted in a grid of small communities, plotted for the convenience of the companies as they serviced the tracks and trains and collected and transported the commodities produced on the land.

But these grant programs meant that food producers were scattered across the countryside. The next generation of land grant acts expanded the granted acreage as settlers moved into the semiarid high plains, where more land was required to support a family. That further isolated food producers from one another and from community centers. A majority of these settlers came from agrarian Europe, where farmers often lived in towns and traveled to their fields to work the land—a communal structure that was replicated from colonial times on the Eastern Seaboard of the United States. The cumulative effect of the immigration and land grant policies shaped a unique communal dynamic. This in turn generated the academic discipline of rural sociology at land grant universities, a field of study quickly adopted by rural religious educational institutions. Events such as the two world wars, numerous regional conflicts with Indigenous people, the Great Depression, and the Dust Bowl affected the sociology of food production and sustainability and ministry. But several concepts from rural sociology are key.

The Importance of Language

A subtle yet significant shift has been taking place in the very language that is used to describe the culture of agriculture. Agriculture is referred to as "food production." Farmers and ranchers are referred to as "food producers." Food is often referred to as a "commodity," something to be bought and sold. This shift in vocabulary fits well into the modern, industrialized, and mechanized food system that has developed in the last century. Those who grow the food are just part of the production chain. Those who need the food are ultimately just consumers. But this shift in language negates the deep connection between community and creation, people and land in the process of feeding everyone who must eat.

Merriam-Webster defines *agriculture* as "the science, art, or practice of cultivating the soil, producing crops, and raising livestock and in varying degrees the preparation and marketing of the resulting product."[2] Poignantly, agriculture is defined not just as a science (empirical knowledge) but also as an art involving creativity and as a practice—raising something that meets a real need.

Embedded in the word *agriculture* is the word *culture*, which *Merriam-Webster* defines as "the customary beliefs, social forms, and material traits of a racial, religious, or social group; the characteristic features of everyday existence (such as diversions or a way of life) shared by people in a place or time . . . the integrated pattern of human knowledge, belief, and behavior that depends upon the capacity for learning and transmitting knowledge to succeeding generations."[3] And *culture* can also mean "to prepare and use for the raising of crops, to foster the growth of." The word *agri-culture* (*agri* is from the Latin *ager*, meaning "land") implies a connection between people, the land, and growing food. The use of production-and-commodity language undermines that eco-sociological connection and, I would argue, dehumanizes the act of growing food.

Scientists commonly hold that human agriculture, the intentional domestication and cultivation of plants, goes back at least twelve thousand years (though a recent archeological find in Israel suggests the primitive cultivation of wheat and barley may go back twenty-three thousand years). Herding or animal husbandry predates crop agriculture by another one thousand years, with the domestication of pigs in Mesopotamia. Thus organized agriculture has existed for at least thirteen millennia.

Pause a moment and contemplate the arrogance of an industry globally redefining a seminal eco-sociological relationship—a relationship that sustains people and impacts the rest of creation—based on a food production system that has developed in just the past century. As noted previously, a new lexicon has developed that renames what had once been a land culture in terms of an industrialized food production system. The lexicon we use is critical. As Mark Pagel states, "The words we use—and how we use them—matter immensely because they shape the way we perceive the world and participate within it."[4] This shift in the language we use to describe how and from where our food comes to our table contributes to reshaping our attitudes about food and sustainability—moving the focus from agri-*culture* to agri-*business*. As Wendell Berry stresses, this comes with a dreadful impact on society. Regarding the shift from agriculture to agribusiness, he asserts,

> Its influence on us may already have been disastrous, and we have not yet seen the worst. . . . It is the work of the institutions of agriculture: the experts and the agri-businessmen, who have promoted so-called efficiency at the expense of community, and quantity at the expense of quality. The result is that the life of the land, which in its native processes is infinite, has been made totally dependent upon the finite, scarce and expensive materials and products of industry. The result is the disuse of so-called marginal lands, potentially productive, but dependent upon intensive human care and long-term human familiarity and affection. The result is the virtual destruction of the farm culture without which farming, in any but the exploitive and extractive sense, is impossible.[5]

Berry goes on to underscore that food needs to be understood culturally:

> My point is that food is a cultural, not a technological, product. (That is, I'm saying that culture then is a larger category than technology and includes technology.) A culture is not a collection of relics or ornaments, but a practical necessity, and its destruction invokes calamity. A healthy culture is a communal order of memory, insight, value, and aspiration. It would reveal the human necessities and the human limits. It would clarify our

inescapable bonds to the earth and to each other. It would assure that the necessary restraints be observed, that the necessary work be done, and that it be done well. A healthy *farm* culture can only be based upon familiarity; it can only grow among a people soundly established upon the land; it would nourish and protect a human intelligence of the land that no amount of technology can satisfactorily replace.[6]

I strongly concur. And using the language of agri*culture* rather than agribusiness is key in forming and communicating our perceptions and attitudes regarding food and sustainability.

The Importance of History

Culture develops over time in an interaction between a community and a place. Hence, culture is shaped by history even as it is lived out in the present. As Martin Luther King Jr. said in *The Strength to Love*, "We are not makers of history. We are made by history."[7] I touch on just a few specific historical events in this book. But it is important to acknowledge the significance of history in a community and culture of growing food. Lawrence W. Farris states this well in his book *Dynamics of Small Town Ministry*:

Understanding the small town's history is essential for a number of reasons. As its residents meet the present and confront the future, they do so out of an indwelling sense of the past, a living story that is widely shared and cherished. History is alive, active, and oral in ways not often found outside small towns. . . . The town's present reality has evolved from how and why it began, from the challenges it has met, from the traditions that have grown over time, and from the sharing of all this history from generation to generation. The lower mobility of small-town residents allows them to live into the history of the place even as they share in writing new chapters.[8]

In such a context, where a lot of food is grown, there are often multigenerational relationships between family groups and institutions such as schools and churches. Communal memory is long. History shapes communal identity. Of course, history can also be a burden. Refrains such as "We've never done it that way before" or "We tried that, but it didn't work" can be roadblocks. Also, the historic memory of engaging issues in a way that became painful and divisive in the community lingers and creates a shared reticence about entering into such discourse again.

Hence, as it pertains specifically to the subject of food and sustainability, that historic communal memory matters because history can shape even the willingness to engage in discussion around potentially controversial topics like injustices in the food system. Harkening back to the flood year of 1993, I recall listening to a surprisingly heated call-in discussion on public radio about contributing factors to the flood. Epic rains in southwestern Minnesota had flooded the Minnesota River, which was surging into the junction with the Mississippi River at St. Paul. The floodwaters continued to wreak havoc all down the Mississippi River basin, breaching levees and flooding fields, towns, and cities. Metropolitan people were dealing with road closures and extended commutes due to the floodwaters. One frustrated St. Paul resident said (this is a paraphrase), "Those farmers in rural Minnesota are draining their fields and sending their water at me. Why do we let them do that?" The caller was angry, but I give the gentleman credit for knowing something about field tiling. This is a technique whereby perforated plastic pipe, called tile line, is placed in the ground in low-lying sections of a farm field to drain off excess water. It is a proven drainage practice that dates back to the Roman Empire and has been used in the United States since the early 1800s.

What the caller was not accounting for was the fact that farmers were following what were considered best practices. In the 1970s, tiling had been promoted as a part of agricultural policy. Under the Nixon administration and the leadership of US Department of Agriculture (USDA) secretary Earl Butz, a policy of "get big or get out" encouraged large farming operations to put as much tillable land into food production as possible, "farming fence row to fence row." Administration policy included rolling back many Roosevelt-era conservation and subsidy programs that grew out of the Great Depression economic disaster, which began in 1929, and the Dust Bowl ecological disaster. New Deal policies had included subsidies to fallow land, especially land that shouldn't have been cultivated in the first place, in an effort to keep the soil in place, manage supply and demand, and stabilize prices.

The Nixon administration flipped that approach and subsidized farmers to put more land into production in anticipation of potential grain deals with China and the Soviet Union. This was coupled with a land-boom mentality in which financial institutions flush with cash encouraged farmers to acquire more land by borrowing money at high interest rates against their current capital assets with the hope of making huge profits due to rising land prices. One farmer who I have come to count as a friend said, "The banker put his hand on my shoulder, showed me my asset summary, and said, 'Jim, you're a millionaire. I think you should buy more land.'" Now, Jim is quick to say that he was free to decide. He wasn't coerced. But it was the era of "get big or get out," and he was a millionaire on paper. And then the agricultural economy went bad—unbelievably bad. The international grain deals fell through, land value collapsed, loan collateral evaporated, lenders called the notes, and Jim and many others like him lost it all. And thus the 1980s farm crisis was born. In the late 2010s, amid international tariffs and trade wars, the people most impacted by the shifting winds of public policy did not forget the failures of past administrations.

Flash back to that call-in discussion on public radio in late 1993: "Those farmers in rural Minnesota are draining their fields and sending their water at me. Why do we let them do that?" Try to hear that through the filter of a farm family who has lived in a place through the Great Depression and Dust Bowl and through government programs that say first "Don't plant that land" and then "Drain and plant that land" to post-1993, with federal agencies saying, "You should probably break the tile that we paid you to install and stop draining the land." What I heard from the people I served was a sense of betrayal by and mistrust of policy makers in the state capital and Washington, DC. When the rural people I knew spoke of these matters, their language would often devolve into "us and them" rhetoric. "Those people" in Washington or Chicago or St. Paul do not understand what we are going through. The folks on the land had not forgotten the history of these policies and what happened in the 1930s, '40s, '70s, and '80s and again in 1993, and the way those changing policies were characterized by "outsiders" made them wary of anyone, including pastors, who engaged in conversation about farming and sustainability.

One farmer I know is keenly aware of the history of public policy regarding agriculture. He and I disagree on many things, but we have found a way to have a civil debate over the issues of farming practices and land sustainability. He has taught me much about how he runs his operation and why he makes certain choices. But he has conceded some points to me from the perspective of a consumer who cares about where and how food is grown. Whenever I teach a course on this topic, I invite him to interact with the students. For that, I have gained his respect. To be honest, he would rather that pastors and seminary teachers like myself stay out of the conversation concerning agricultural practices and policy and "stick to preaching and teaching the Bible." I've countered with the fact that the Bible says a lot about these issues, but that remains an ongoing part of our conversation. He is a beef producer, to use the parlance of the industry, and has been a lobbyist for beef producers in the state capital. His is a century farm, meaning it has been in his family for more than one hundred years. He is the third generation on his family farm, and the fourth generation is now partnering with him and will take over when he retires. He likes to talk about "cubical thinking" by regulators at the state capital and in Washington, DC. And he would be more than happy to recite a long list of policy and regulation decisions that were ill conceived because they were not based on the current science of food production.

Many farmers lost their entire crop in 1993. Yes, many had crop insurance. And there was the Zero-92 government aid program. But those were just life preservers in the flood. No one made money; many lost it. Again, going back to the story that opens this chapter, recall the farmer who owned the field adjacent to SHF. He said, "For thirty years I have farmed that piece of land and have taken what the Lord has given me—good or bad, mostly good. Now I am supposed to tell the Lord it's not good enough and plow it under and take the government money. Pastor Mark, I just can't do it." I talked with him again when he was planting the next spring. He said, "Pastor, remember the conversation we had last fall? Well, I decided not to take the government payment, and I harvested this field. I broke even. I thought you might like to know that." When his livelihood and his family's well-being were at stake, he made a decision based on his own history with that piece of land and his faith. When he and his wife decided to retire from farming, they opted to sell those fields to SHF. They would have made a lot more money selling the land to a larger farming enterprise. But they wanted the land cared for like they, and her father before them, had cared for it. Faith in God and their history with those farm fields were more important than money.

Of course, the root cause of the floods of 1993 was not field tiling but global climate change, one of the key issues impacting food and sustainability that I named in chapter 1. The scientific community has been talking about this reality for more than a century. But in 1993, it was not a common component of the public discussion. The frequency of flooding events, one-hundred- and five-hundred-year floods, has increased dramatically in recent years, causing the US Geological Service to rethink its prediction models. For example, from 2015 to 2017, Houston had three consecutive five-hundred-year floods.[9] Climatologists attribute the severity of these events and their growing frequency to climate change. History matters in this way, too, as food growers seek to reorient their historical practices to rapidly changing ecosystems and adopt methods and technology that do not worsen the impact of the changing climate.

Many great minds have reflected on the ongoing influence of history in shaping our present and future. Nobel– and Pulitzer Prize–winning author William Faulkner famously wrote, "The past is never dead. It's not even past." William Shakespeare penned, "What is past is prologue," a quotation that is carved into the National Archives Building in Washington, DC. History matters. Particularly for those who grow our food, the multigenerational history and communal memory related to their vocation and their relationships, familial and communal, shape how they engage present realities and anticipate the future. For their sake, and the sake of fruitful discourse, history needs to be taken into account in engaging the issues concerning food and sustainability.

The Importance of Place

Another major aspect of the sociology of rural communities is the significance of place. Kent Hunter, a church growth consultant, speaks to this in his *The Lord's Harvest and the Rural Church: A New Look at Ministry in the Agri-culture.* Hunter asserts that community happens differently in metropolitan and small-town and rural contexts. I will address the contrast with the metropolitan context later in the chapter. In a rural context, community tends to center on place. Often, you will interact with a high percentage of the people you know from church at the grocery store, the basketball game, the Zumba class, the school board meeting, or the local café. Communities of interest overlap in a community based on geography. Often, these connections to place are multigenerational. People migrate through small rural communities, but those who stay often have deep communal and familial roots in that place. This can impact communication. Conflict is often avoided due to the reverberations it can have throughout a smaller community.[10]

Place becomes personal in this context. Home and vocation overlap. Whether farm or ranch or fishing village, the places where our food is produced are the loci of both life and livelihood for multitudes of families in small-town and rural communities. As noted, many of those families have multigenerational connections to those places. When economic turmoil threatens, it is particularly traumatic for those families and their communities. When I started pastoral ministry during the 1980s farm crisis, suicide, attempted suicide, and threatened suicide were the most prevalent urgent pastoral care issues with which I dealt. A 2017 article by the *Guardian* reports on a 2016 study by the Centers for Disease Control and Prevention (CDC), which found that people working in agriculture—including farmers, farm laborers, ranchers, fishers, and lumber harvesters—die by suicide at a rate higher than any other occupation. The data suggested that the suicide rate for agricultural workers in seventeen states was nearly five times higher than the general population. This is not just a US phenomenon. The *Guardian* article states, "The US farmer suicide crisis echoes a much larger farmer suicide crisis happening globally: an Australian farmer dies by suicide every four days; in the UK, one farmer a week takes his or her own life; in France, one farmer dies by suicide every two days; in India, more than 270,000 farmers have died by suicide since 1995."[11] The CDC study emphasizes that farming-related factors—such as weather, interest rates, and commodity prices—are stressful and beyond the farmers' control. I would argue from my experience that the risk of being the one who loses the family farm—home, often for multiple generations of a family, and source of livelihood—is another huge factor.

During one rural immersion experience I was leading for seminary professors, one of the participants, a PhD, asked a cutting question of a farmer after hearing about his trials and tribulations with farming: "If it's so hard, why don't you just give it up and get a job in the city? A business person in the city, if they can't make it, they close it up and do something else." The question was extremely blunt. But it was also an excellent query because it verbalized what others were thinking and gave the farmer an opportunity to articulate his deep connection to the land, the soil, his family's place. Without hesitation, the farmer responded, "This land has belonged to my family for three generations. Growing food to feed the world is what I do. The soil is in my blood. I can't walk away from it."

J. B. Jackson, whom the *New York Times* once called "America's greatest living writer on the forces that have shaped the land this nation occupies,"[12] wrote in *Discovering the Vernacular of Landscape*, "It is place, permanent position in both the social and topographical sense, that gives us our identity." That social and physical connection to place is foundational for people in rural places who grow our food and tend the land that produces it.

The Importance of Story and Relationship

As noted in the introduction, the writings of Tex Sample (yes, Tex is his given name) provide wonderful insights into the sociology of food-growing communities. Sample is ordained in the United Methodist Church, has two doctorates, and taught for thirty-two years at the St. Paul School of Theology in Kansas City, Missouri. If you peruse his bibliography, you will see he likely categorizes himself as a "blue-collar" sociologist with titles like *Blue-Collar Ministry: Facing Economic and Social Realities of Working People*, *Hard Living People and Mainstream Christians*, and *Blue-Collar Resistance and the Politics of Jesus*. When I read Sample's book *Ministry in an Oral Culture: Living with Will Rogers, Uncle Remus, and Minnie Pearl*, I had two stark realizations. First, he was describing the people I was called to serve in small-town and rural Minnesota. Second, though I come from a suburban metropolitan background, I was raised in an oral culture. By the latter, I mean that my identity in my family was shaped by story. My mother was a clerk/accountant, and my father was a diesel mechanic, each with a high school diploma. When we gathered for holidays, when we sat around the table for an ordinary meal, when we played board games or card games, we told stories. Those stories communicated practical information, wisdom, and identity. My mother advanced my reading level, without any teacher training, by reading novels out loud with me. She would read a chapter, and then I would read a chapter. I strongly suspect this influenced my decision to get an undergraduate degree in English literature.

Sample makes a distinction between oral culture and literate culture. He is careful to note that a person from an oral culture is not illiterate but rather uses a narrative-based orality for learning and teaching, processing information, and making decisions. He asserts,

> It is my contention that about half of the people in the United States are people who work primarily out of a traditional orality, by which I mean a people who can read and write—though some cannot—but those whose appropriation and engagement with life is oral. More than this, I am convinced that most churches have a clear majority of the membership who work from a traditional orality. When one moves outside the United States into most of the rest of the world, the mass of oral cultures, both primary and

traditional, looms even larger. Two-thirds of the people in the world are oral.[13]

Not only are a majority of Anglo-Americans involved in food production shaped by this oral culture, but so are a majority of new immigrant populations who grow and harvest food and work in large livestock operations and food processing plants. In addition, if Sample's assertion is true, and I believe it is, a high percentage of the general population is shaped by orality. People from an oral culture do not discuss issues of food and sustainability. These topics are the focus of primarily literate sources, such as scientific studies, government publications, or academic books.

Perhaps the main entrance to discussion with a person from an oral culture is through the door of story. "An oral culture lives by storytelling," says Sample.[14] He also states, "Oral people think in relationships."[15] And this relational nature is key to how justice and social change are engaged: "When people think in proverbs, stories, and relationships, they do not 'do' critique. . . . It helps to understand relational thinking in contrast to that of a more abstract conceptual kind. . . . An issue that comes up will be considered in terms of the family and communal ties one has. A moral issue will be considered in the light of these same kinship and local connections. Any attempt at social change will need to be grounded in such relationships, and religious beliefs will be understood much more in relational than discursive ways."[16]

I experienced numerous examples of this while serving as a pastor. My denomination has produced social statements on a wide range of topics, including abortion, care of creation, genetics, economics, and human sexuality. I always served in a more sociopolitically conservative setting. These social statements are well crafted but tend to be formed from a literate perspective. They are also more moderate in their assumptions than the people in the conservative ministries I served preferred. Hence, they were controversial. When I discussed them with congregation members and leaders, and if the conversation remained on a theoretical, propositional plain, it was contentious, and we had difficulty coming to some level of mutual understanding. When story and relationship entered the conversation, however, the tenor of the discussion changed.

An example was the Evangelical Lutheran Church in America (ELCA) 1991 social statement on abortion. Obviously, this issue is not food and sustainability related. But the way we needed to address it in a highly relational, oral culture applies to issues of sustainability and food. When discussing this denominational declaration with church leaders, there was considerable pushback. This was a politically conservative context with a strong pro-life focus. It wasn't until the treasurer of this small congregation had the courage to tell the story of her niece, who had been raped and made the decision to terminate the pregnancy—a story she told in tears—that the whole conversation changed. I learned from that experience and applied it to conversations about what it means to grow food and tend the land. We have experts in food production and in the ecology of the land who produce scientific papers addressed to colleagues in their field. But these issues are not just about the science; they are also about the story of the land and its people. They are about relationships, not just the economics of global food production.

The Rural-Urban Divide

In 2007, a quiet yet momentous event took place. For the first time in human history, the world's population became majority urban. Let that sink in. Until that year, for all human history, more people on the planet lived in rural contexts than urban ones. That change came somewhat earlier in US history, recognized with the 1920 census. Until the mid-1800s in the United States, urban centers were not far removed from the surrounding rural countryside, which supplied needed food and raw materials for the industry of the time. There was more common understanding and common cause between the two groups. That began to change dramatically with the onset of the Second Industrial Revolution in the latter half of the nineteenth century, as more and more people were needed to work in urban-based factories.

Now we speak of the rural-urban divide. This divide is not just a geographic one; it is political, economic, and sociological as well. In the United States, approximately 97 percent of the geography and 20 percent of the population are rural. In our political system, rural people often perceive themselves to be underrepresented in federal and state government. The degree to which this perception is fact can be debated. All states have equal numbers of senators on the federal level. It can be argued that the more sparsely populated, more rural states are therefore overrepresented in the senate. Yet many US congressional districts have some rural areas and some urban areas, depending on how the district lines are drawn. In the 114th Congress (2015–16), for example, only 34 of the 435 districts were more than 50 percent rural. This means that only 8 percent of the house districts were majority rural. Metropolitan-based legislators are seen to pass laws that impact rural people without needing to attend to the opinions of the rural citizens. This perception of government disconnect contributes to a sense of division and suspicion on the part of rural people. The United States has an economic divide as well. Despite popular perceptions, the percentages of people in poverty in the United States are higher in rural areas than in urban ones. In addition, most new jobs are created in metropolitan areas. This increases the outward migration of people from rural areas to urban centers. According to the World Bank, 78 percent of the world's poor people live in rural areas and work mainly in agriculture.[17]

Throughout my life, I have noted that some of the most interesting rural-urban differences are cultural or sociological. For example, urban people have a different orientation to space and place.[18] Shaped by a more densely populated setting, with more built rather than natural environment, urban dwellers tend to maintain a smaller personal space. They can maneuver more comfortably in crowded spaces like busy streets, malls, and the like. I have witnessed rural people become disoriented in crowded city environments and experience a slight claustrophobic reaction. Conversely, I have witnessed city dwellers in a rural context say things like "My goodness, there is nothing out here!" as they gaze over thousands of acres of farm fields and have a minor agoraphobic spell. As noted earlier, Kent Hunter asserts that community forms around shared place in a rural context. But in a metropolitan context, Hunter contends that community forms around interests. People are willing to travel outside their immediate community to meet their needs for retail shopping or work and to fulfill their interests at an exercise club or church. So in a more densely populated area, an individual has an immediate neighborhood and multiple additional communities built around work, school, recreation, church, politics, and other communities of interest. And the people in each of those communities may have little or no overlap. Something you say or do in one community likely will never be known in your other communities of interest—unlike in a rural context, where communities of interest overlap in a common place, it is possible that everyone will know.

For example, three years into my first call, our family had grown to four. We had two young children. We felt like we would be staying for a while, so we purchased one of those large wooden play sets to erect in the backyard of the parsonage. One day, at 9:00 in the morning, it was delivered unassembled to the parsonage in a panel truck that backed up to the garage, where the play set was off-loaded. I had a haircut appointment that afternoon at 3:00 at a salon in the next town, eight miles away. When I arrived, I discovered my stylist was one of my parishioners. She escorted me to the chair. I sat down, and she curtly snapped the apron around my neck and said with a hint of anger, "So, Pastor, I hear you're leaving us." I was dumbfounded and stammered, "What?" She responded, "Someone saw a moving van in the driveway of the parsonage this morning, and everyone is saying that you must have taken a new call." Suddenly her behavior made sense. I laughed and said, "Wait till you see what I put up in the backyard. Then you'll know we're not planning on going anywhere any time soon." She was reassured, but the message was out. In less than six hours, the incorrect news that I was leaving had traveled eight miles and had found its way to hairdressers, the equivalent of the operator's exchange for the old telephone party lines. Fortunately, I was able to speak to the operator directly before things got out of hand.

Also based on my experience, I have noted a difference in the sense of time between rural and metropolitan people. Though this is not universally true, I do observe that metropolitan people tend to function more by *chronos* (chronological or sequential) time. Rural people pay attention to clocks and calendars as well, but many are also significantly affected by *kairos* time. *Kairos* refers to moments of opportunity regardless of calendar or clock. The significance of relationship and many rural vocations' closer connection to the rhythms of creation contribute to the influence of *kairos* time. I found that no matter the size of the agenda for a meeting, people came expecting to spend two hours together, with fellowship at the end. A metropolitan person may want to focus on the agenda, honoring people's time, and complete the meeting as efficiently as possible. The default model for decision-making in a rural context is consensus building. Consensus building also often takes more time than the simple majority vote decision model. Folks are willing to take time in decision-making to maintain relationships. The final vote is often an affirmation of the consensus already established. With fewer people, that method is viable. With larger numbers, simple majority votes are more efficient. I have witnessed clergy who come from metropolitan backgrounds but are serving in rural communities experience conflict over cultural nuance. In identifying the differing emphasis on time, I do not intend to imply that one is better than the other. Rather, I offer this observation as an encouragement for leaders to recognize and honor the differences.

One congregation I served needed more sanctuary space and a kitchen renovation because it was growing. This would require changing the architectural profile of a church that hadn't been altered since it was built in the 1890s. The leaders went to work engaging the congregation, drawing up blueprints, and creating a financial plan. Several congregational meetings were held along the way. When it came time for the final approval vote, there were only three dissenting ballots. I expected the next council meeting to be the start of the implementation phase. But our congregational president said, "I think we need to slow down. We're moving too fast." Even though the vote was anonymous, the leaders knew who had cast the three nos. They were descendants of two pillar families, one whose great-grandfather had donated the land upon which the church was built. The leaders were willing to take more time to speak with them, address their specific concerns, and ensure that going ahead with the project would not fracture their relationship with the congregation. And it worked. All three eventually became proponents of the renovation, and three years later, all debt for the project was paid.

Though urban and rural people are all stakeholders in the need for food and sustainability, they often differ on how best to produce food and create a food system that is sustainable economically and environmentally. For many producers, where and how food is produced is a first-order concern. Food production is their livelihood, and its site is also their home. As noted earlier, that place may have been in their family for multiple generations. If the farm or ranch isn't sustainable, the impacts on their lives are huge. So undergirding the many facets of how food is produced are significant decisions made every day by food producers. One might ask, In times of lower prices, do I use chemical fertilizers to increase production to try to break even? Do I irrigate in times of drought? Can I afford to put land into conservation reserve which might be good for the environment, but might result in my inability to pay my bills? Producers are also impacted by the multitude of decisions made beyond the farm or ranch and beyond their control—matters of public policy, market volatility, and global economics, which, to some degree, can dictate how they produce food.

For urban dwellers, the concerns are more second order, "many steps removed from direct contact with the land."[19] Most do not grow food, but all consume it. Many have concerns regarding their foods' nutrition, safety, availability, and affordability. Some are concerned about where their food comes from and how it is raised and how those factors impact the health and sustainability of the environment. Those who can afford more than just the cheapest food available affect these issues by how they spend their food dollars, opting to buy organic products or food that is produced in what is termed as "environmentally friendly" ways and hence supporting such practices. Some urban dwellers, for good reasons, actively support organizations such as the American Society for the Prevention of Cruelty to Animals (ASPCA) or Greenpeace, which challenge agricultural practices deemed to be harmful to animals or the environment.

The different perspectives between rural and urban dwellers around food production and how the land should be sustained can contribute to the rural-urban divide and even devolve into adversarial attitudes. I have heard rural people characterize their urban counterparts as follows: "They are interfering in things they know nothing about, telling us how to farm and ranch, and they haven't even seen a real farm or ranch. All they want is cheap food, and they don't care about us who grow it." I have heard urban people characterize their rural counterparts as backward and not caring about the future. They have also accused farmers and ranchers of raising food as fast and as cheaply as possible to make more money, polluting the land and water in the process. If an adversarial rural-urban divide prevails, that will undermine our ability as a society to constructively address the food and sustainability issues that impact all of us who must eat.

Other major stakeholders in food production and sustainability are food processing companies, which take the largest percentage of the food dollar and tend to control the marketing of food. Marketing is sometimes employed to give the appearance that food is being produced in ways that are more palatable to consumers or that ensure quality. For instance, if you pay attention to the packaging of certain products in the grocery store, you will see nostalgic depictions of agriculture: animals roaming the rolling hills of green pastures, poultry pecking peacefully in a classic barnyard. Modern agriculture looks very different. More and more food is being raised in less and less space—hard work and messy business, especially when managing animal waste. Thus, this type of marketing, though it sells food, exacerbates the divide of understanding between the rural food producer and the urban food consumer.

Labeling can also be misleading. For example, some milk products have a label that proclaims "No Antibiotics." By law, bulk milk is tested at the farm and again at the plant. If any antibiotics are detected, the whole load is discarded at the expense of the farmer. But that doesn't mean the milk came from a cow that has never been treated with antibiotics. If a dairy cow gets sick, it will be treated rather than left to suffer and die. The animal is separated from the herd until the antibiotic is out of its system and the milk tests antibiotic-free. An "Organic" label means something different. Organic milk comes from animals that have never been treated with antibiotics or hormones and that have been fed only organic feed. If an organic producer must treat an animal, that cow is either sold to a conventional dairy or processed for meat. Labels like "Certified Black Angus Beef," "Cage-Free," and "Free Range" don't necessarily mean what many consumers think they mean. Food processors, wholesalers, and retailers are happy to allow us to purchase our food based on such misconceptions if doing so means they will receive price premiums for food so labeled. Again, this worsens the divide of understanding between the rural food producer and the urban food consumer.

It seems apparent to me that the best way to address the rural-urban divide is to build bridges. The truth of the matter is that urban dwellers influence the food and sustainability system as consumers and voters. Producers and processors need to be responsive to consumers' wishes. For instance, it was consumers who successfully pressured McDonald's to source chicken and eggs from producers that followed more humane practices. Urban consumers can use the power of their vote to influence policy makers. Perhaps the most direct way to impact how food is produced would be to build coalitions between rural producers and urban consumers based on more realistic understandings of the stake each has in the food system. The Christian church is well placed to help facilitate such coalition building. This will be explored in chapter 4.

In the mid-1990s, a TV series called *Christy* ran on CBS. It was a historical drama based in the fictional twentieth-century community of Cutter Gap in the Appalachian Mountains of Tennessee. The story revolves around a Christian mission in the community and three main characters: Christy Huddleston, a young, educated woman from the city who comes to teach in the mission school; Rev. David Grantland, a young minister from Boston; and Alice Henderson, an older, wiser Quaker missionary who does service ministry in the mission's parish. Cutter Gap is a community of people who live close to the land. The series is well done, wholesome, though a bit nostalgic. I was captivated by the fifth episode, "A Closer Walk," in which the schoolhouse is burned down in a suspected arson. Someone in the community is pushing back against the "uppity city ways" being taught to the children of the Gap. There are two subplots. Rev. David, a young man unfamiliar with the ways of the mountain people, takes a heavy-handed approach to leading the men of the Gap in rebuilding the school-house. Eventually, he is challenged and publicly humiliated by an older man whom he has crossed. To add insult to injury, David gets caught up in seminary speak while trying to assure a ninety-two-year-old dying woman of the promise of eternal life. David feels shamed and ineffective and wants to leave. Meanwhile, Christy comes up with a social service idea for the women of the Gap to make quilts and weavings to sell in the city to help support their families. The idea, though well intended, is not well received because it does not consider the difference in gender roles in that mountain community compared to the city from which Christy originates. The issues come to some level of resolution when, with the help of Miss Alice, both David and Christy realize that they were not sent to Cutter Gap to fix the people there. Rather, they are there to become part of the community—to teach, to learn, and to build relationships of trust so that together, they can work to better the town.

"A Closer Walk" has become a valuable teaching tool for me, even though it is based on life in a hundred-year-old community. It highlights the cross-cultural nature of the interaction between rural and urban. Yes, the rural-urban divide is real, and it appears to be growing, spurred on by mutual misunderstanding and mistrust. The relationship between urban and rural has devolved into a competition for resources and influence. A growing divide will serve neither community well. The reality is, rural and urban communities need each other. Urban dwellers need the food and other raw commodities that are produced primarily in rural places. Rural dwellers need markets for the goods they produce as well as the finished products that are processed or manufactured largely in urban places. Most germane to the focus of this book, everyone, urban or rural, has a stake in the sustainability of our common home—earth. And of course, everyone, rural or urban, must eat. Rather than participating in a growing divide, people of faith should answer the call to bridge the divide for the common good. The biblical and theological scaffolding for this will be the topic of the next chapter.

Questions for Reflection and Discussion

1. How has the power of story played a role in your life? What role has it played in your congregation or parish?

2. Have you found history to be more of a hindrance or an asset to mission and ministry?

3. To what extent are you influenced by *kairos* time? How about your congregation or parish?

4. What side of the urban-rural divide do you stand on? From where you stand, what is your perspective of the other side?

5. What is your stake in the food and sustainability system? Does your congregation or parish have a stake in the system? If so, what is it?

3

"And God Saw
That It Was Good"

Biblical and Theological Connections

Early in my first call as a pastor, I was studying the texts for preaching that Sunday. The appointed Old Testament lectionary reading was from Isaiah 5:1–7. This is basically a prophetic parable that equates the "house" of Israel with a vineyard that is producing bad grapes. The appointed text ends with "For the vineyard of the Lord of hosts is the house of Israel, and the people of Judah are his pleasant planting; he expected justice, but saw bloodshed; righteousness, but heard a cry!" (Isa 5:7). I recognized this was an agricultural reference with social justice implications.

My excellent biblical teachers schooled me to read the larger context of the passage beyond the lectionary text. And so I read on: "Ah, you who join house to house, who add field to field, until there is room for no one but you, and you are left to live alone in the midst of the land! The Lord of hosts has sworn in my hearing: Surely many houses shall be desolate, large and beautiful houses, without inhabitant. For ten acres of vineyard shall yield but one bath, and a homer of seed shall yield a mere ephah" (Isa 5:8–10). I was stunned. This eighth-century BCE Scripture was describing the challenge of the people I had been called to serve.

Traversing nearly three thousand years, this verse spoke to me: "Ah, you who join house to house, who add field to field, until there is room for no one but you, and you are left to live alone in the midst of the land!" On the twenty-mile drive I made regularly along a county highway from the parsonage to the smaller open-country congregation, I passed eight abandoned farm sites. Each one of those places had represented a family, perhaps several generations of it. Each deserted site was a silent witness of farm foreclosures, farm auctions, and farmer suicides. The farmhouses—each with two dark, empty second-story windows—looked to me like square, blank, staring skulls. Today, all those abandoned farmsteads are gone. One would never even know they existed. They were bull-dozed and turned into a few more acres of farmland purchased by another farmer in the process of adding house to house and field to field. But I have been in many other agricultural settings, even internationally, and I have seen many, many other empty, dark, staring skeletons. "Ah, you who add house to house and field to field"—the prophetic implications of this one text continue to speak to those who seek to sustain the land and sustain their livelihoods by growing food in the twenty-first century.

In encountering this text, I realized God cared about what was happening on the land and to the people of the land. That was true in the eighth century BCE and, presumably, is true today. God cares about the issues that impacted the people I served. That caring is multilayered. Certainly, this text carries a metanarrative of prophetic condemnation for the social injustices and theological transgressions of the house of Israel and the people of Judah. But there is also a layer of care for individual farmers who are displaced from the land by said injustices. And even the productivity and fertility of the land itself is a matter of concern to God. All this in these ten verses. Thus began my journey to understand more deeply the context of this Scripture and others that speak to the realities of food, sustainability, and ministry.

In this chapter, we will explore some basic theological concepts undergirded with key biblical verses and narratives. There will be a heavy emphasis on the Old Testament because that is where a predominance of scriptural material speaking to food and sustainability resides. The selection of texts is by no means all encompassing; there are numerous other possibilities. I encourage you to seek them out and engage them. Let us begin in the beginning.

God Is the Creator and Claims the Creation

The assertion that God creates and claims creation may sound self-evident, but it is also radical and foundational. There is a reason Scripture begins with "In the beginning when God created the heavens and the earth" (Gen 1:1). This concept is foundational to God's authority to speak: "Thus says God, the Lord, who created the heavens and stretched them out, who spread out the earth and what comes from it, who gives breath to the people upon it and spirit to those who walk in it" (Isa 42:5). God's claim as creator is foundational to the first article of our historic Christian creeds, our core statements of faith. In the Apostle's Creed, we profess, "I believe in God, the Father Almighty, creator of Heaven and earth." And in the Nicene Creed, we confess, "We believe in one God, the Father, the Almighty, maker of heaven and earth, of all that is, seen and unseen."

And the creator claims the creation: "The earth is the Lord's and all that is in it, the world, and those who live in it" (Ps 24:1). We have also, "The land shall not be sold in perpetuity, for the land is mine; with me you are but aliens and tenants" (Lev 25:23). There is no place in Scripture where God relinquishes that claim. When we, as Christian leaders, engage the issues of food and sustainability, the word *creation* needs to be a part of the conversation. This is important because *creation* connotes a faith-based relationship to the creator God that terms like *environment* and *ecosystem* do not. As Old Testament scholar Walter Brueggemann asserts, "The whole cluster of words—creator/creation/create/creature—are confessional words freighted with peculiar meaning. Terms such as 'cosmos' and 'nature' should never be carelessly used as equivalents, for these words do not touch the theocentric, covenantal relational affirmation being made. The word 'creation' belongs inevitably with its counter word 'creator.' . . . The single sentence, 'Creator creates creation,' is decisive for everything. . . . This governing sentence affirms that the creator is not disinterested and the creation is not autonomous."[1]

What we as ministry leaders bring to the conversation of food and sustainability is a Judeo-Christian, biblical-theological perspective. That perspective doesn't need to conflict with science, but it is not purely empirical or scientific, and it is not disengaged from the ethical implications of food and sustainability. As Brueggemann notes, the term *creation* implies a creator, someone other than us, to whom we as people of faith are accountable. Unfortunately, some extremist Christian groups have co-opted the concept of creation and set it against science. This has caused some in the secular scientific community to label any reference to creation in a discussion of the issues of sustainability and food as "creationism" promoted by "creationists." But a faithful, biblical-theological understanding of God as creator claiming creation does not need to be mutually exclusive of empirical, scientific knowledge. Mainline Christians need to reclaim the word *creation* as a part of the conversation regarding food and sustainability. This foundational concept permeates all the major categories of Old Testament literature: the Pentateuch, the wisdom literature, the historical books, and the prophets. Fundamentally, the Old Testament assertion, with various nuances, is that God has created both the land and people and still claims them.

There is a second concept that is ancillary to the premise of God's claim as creator: God shares responsibility for the land with people, who are still a part of creation. In a lovely Hebrew pun embedded in the second creation story in Genesis 2, *adam*, the human, is created from *adamah*, the ground. Hence the admonition as the first humans were expelled from the garden of Eden, "By the sweat of your face you shall eat bread until you return to the ground, for out of it you were taken; you are dust, and to dust you shall return" (Gen 3:19). This is something Christians are reminded of on Ash Wednesday and at a Christian burial.

These seemingly self-evident, key creation concepts are nonetheless radical in at least two ways. First, whereas Judaism, Christianity, and Islam are often perceived as competing and even conflicting, the basic creation narrative is unifying for Jews, Christians, and Muslims. Judaism and Christianity share the Hebrew Scriptures, which include Genesis. The Qur'an, the holy book of Islam, includes a parallel creation narrative. The three major monotheistic world religions share this foundational concept. This can be a starting point for interreligious collaboration concerning the common global issues of food and sustainability. In 2014, the Interfaith Center for Sustainable Development organized a conference in Jerusalem on faith and ecology, bringing together clergy and theological students from the Muslim, Jewish, and Christian traditions. Imam Wisam Barhum asserted, "In Islam, the earth is the place that God chose so that people can use it for worship. We must preserve this place and keep it the way God created it so man can worship God." Rabbi Yuval Cherlow stated, "Man was created in the image of God. Therefore, he needs to take responsibility for the world. We must work on perfecting the world, as part of our connection to God." Bishop William Shomali added, "This is a religious issue because it relates to God, who is the creator and asks us to respect the creation. It's also an ethical problem because there are values behind it that we should respect."[2] If this type of dialogue can happen in Jerusalem, we can certainly initiate such conversations in our local communities and broaden those discussions in ways that engender large-scale change.

A second way these creation concepts are radical is that they push back against anthropocentric attitudes about food and sustainability. The belief that God is creator and humans are created—and are, in fact, part of the creation—underscores the theological reality that the creation is not ours to do with however we please. This sets the table for many of the commandments and codes that follow and the subsequent admonishments of the prophets, which I will address later in the chapter. One clear connection with the issues named in chapter 1 relates to genetic manipulation (GM) by humans, especially as it concerns food. Ethicists and theologians have qualms about human beings artificially changing germplasm (the basic building block of life), patenting it, and selling it for profit. They express similar misgivings about the applications of cloning. A phrase you will often hear is that GM is "playing God." If you do an internet search of the phrases "playing God genetics" and "playing God cloning," you will receive over five hundred thousand results, many of them from reputable news media outlets and other organizations. A significant portion of the public debate is framing the ethical questions from a theological perspective. Is this playing God? The corollary question is, Should we be doing this? People of faith understand that we are not God. This core concept of "creator creates creation" certainly encourages these questions. "The earth is the Lord's, and all that is in it, the world, and those who live in it" and "you are dust, and to dust you shall return" should give us pause as we rapidly develop new technologies that impact the sustainability of creation and the very food we eat.

Dominion and "to Till It and Keep It"

In addition to the foundational notion of God as creator claiming creation, some further concepts relate to the previous observations. They are important because historically, they have been used, particularly in Western culture, to justify playing God to some extent. The first is the use of the word *dominion, radah.* Regarding food and sustainability issues, there are two significant occurrences:

> Then God said, "Let us make humankind in our image, according to our likeness; and let them have dominion over the fish of the sea, and over the birds of the air, and over the cattle, and over all the wild animals of the earth, and over every creeping thing that creeps upon the earth." (Gen 1:26)

> You have given them dominion over the works of your hands; you have put all things under their feet, all sheep and oxen, and also the beasts of the field, the birds of the air, and the fish of the sea, whatever passes along the paths of the seas. (Ps 8:6–8)

The limitations of our English translations perhaps invite misuse. A cognate of *dominion* is *dominate.* For a significant part of Judeo-Christian history, some in society seemed to believe that to be given dominion is the same as being given permission to dominate. But some scholars point out that this interpretation misses the original meaning and usage of the Hebrew verb. As Walter Brueggemann notes, "In the now popular indictment of the biblical tradition the notion of human 'subjugation' of earth is blamed for the abuse of nature by way of technology. It is doubtful, however, if that indictment is appropriate. . . . The task of 'dominion' does not have to do with exploitation and abuse. It has to do with securing the well-being of every other creature and bringing the promise of each to full fruition."[3] Scholar James Limburg states, "The ideal model for the relationship between humankind (man and woman) and the earth and its creatures is the king/people relationship. In passages where the same 'have dominion' verb occurs, the emphasis is on gentleness and on an active program of caring that results in shalom."[4]

Similarly, the phrase "to till it and keep it" in Genesis 2:15 is sometimes misconstrued to grant authorization to do with the garden or creation whatever we wish. The verb *keep* in English has a variety of meanings. It can designate retaining something in one's possession or control, as in "to keep the money." It can refer to acting appropriately in relationship to something, as in "to keep a promise." Or it can mean to take care of something, as in "to keep a flock." Reading the first definition into this passage results in a "you till it and it's yours" interpretation. As Limburg notes, "These two words describe the dual task of the farmer and of the entire society. . . . From the beginning, alongside the work of tilling has been the responsibility of 'keeping' the land. This 'keeping' is the same word used to describe the Lord's caring relationship to a city (Ps 127:1) or to a people and an individual (Ps 121). The farmer and the community are called to till the land and to care for it as well."[5]

Historically, there have been attempts to justify humanity's abusive co-opting of the creation based on a shallow reading of texts like those from Genesis 1 and 2 and Psalm 8 noted previously. But in no way does God abdicate God's claim to, involvement in, or care for the creation. The creator seeks to share responsibility with humans in a cocreative relationship—but under God's terms. I would argue that the best way to describe this relationship is as a trust.

Creation as Trust

Frequently, creation is referred to as a gift from God. I would like to challenge that designation. A gift is something given, usually unconditionally, which the recipient now possesses and can decide how to use. God has not transferred unconditional ownership of the creation to human beings. There are conditions to humanity's relationship with the creation. Scholars differ in their views about the best way to characterize that relationship, some making the case for *trust*, others for *gift*. I would argue, however, that trust is more relevant to the relationship we are seeking to describe.

Merriam-Webster defines *trust* as "a charge or duty imposed in faith or confidence or as a condition of some relationship, . . . something committed or entrusted to one to be used or cared for in the interest of another."[6] There are numerous advantages to using the term *trust* rather than *gift* regarding the role of humans in relation to the rest of creation. First, trust implies an ongoing relationship among the creator of the trust, God; the trustees, humans; that which is being placed in trust, creation; and the beneficiaries, all God's creation. Second, *trust* can be faith language. In fact, *trust* is often used synonymously with *faith*, as in "Put your trust [or faith] in the Lord" (Pss 4:5; 9:10). Third, *trust* can be legal language. A trust is a legally binding contract with laws and regulations directing its management. *Covenant* is often used to represent the legal nature of the codes and laws that govern relationships between God and God's people. *Covenant* is defined as "a usually formal, solemn, and binding agreement, and a written agreement or promise usually under seal between two or more parties especially for the performance of some action."[7] However, *covenant* does not express the meaning of caring for something for the sake of another individual, group, or future generations, which I hear intended in the codes and laws especially as they concern food and sustainability. *Gift, covenant, trust*—I don't want to split hairs, but I will choose to use *trust*. With that said, let us explore some of the governing principles, the rules and regulations, of this trust.

Allotment

One of the principles by which this trust is governed is *allotment*, God's distribution of the land to God's people. Related to God's claim in Psalm 24:1, God, as the creator of the trust, determines the rules by which the land is apportioned. Allotment is put forward in Numbers 26:52–56: "The Lord spoke to Moses, saying: To these the land shall be apportioned for inheritance according to the number of names. To a large tribe you shall give a large inheritance, and to a small tribe you shall give a small inheritance; every tribe shall be given its inheritance according to its enrollment. But the land shall be apportioned by lot; according to the names of their ancestral tribes they shall inherit. Their inheritance shall be apportioned according to lot between the larger and the smaller."

Allotment is then echoed in Deuteronomy 19:14: "You must not move your neighbor's boundary marker, set up by former generations, on the property that will be allotted to you in the land that the Lord your God is giving you to possess." On one level, these biblical codes are a matter of practical logistics, establishing an orderly process by which the land is distributed and boundaries are maintained. But a deeper principle is at work as well. As the people finally enter the Promised Land, lest anyone forget, God is still in charge. This land is still God's land, and God has a broader perspective on the land than merely to whom it is allotted. All must benefit from the land. This is a matter of justice and righteousness. As Old Testament scholar Patrick Miller states,

> All members of the community must have access to the benefits and produce of the good land that comes as God's gift. If some do not benefit as much as others, special provisions in the order of society must be set to ensure their wellbeing. The Deuteronomist clearly recognizes that some will benefit more from God's gift than others, but insists that others in the community be provided for. . . .

Life and land are dependent on the firm adherence to righteousness and justice. . . . The mode of living demanded of those who would receive and enjoy the divine gift is characterized by the effort to ensure that all who live in the land shall be treated justly.[8]

By reserving claim to the land, even in its allotment, God can ensure that justice is part of the trust.

Sustainability

The principle of sustainability finds expression in the laws of sabbath and jubilee. Sabbath is not only for worship; it is also for rest. And the list of beneficiaries of this rest is quite comprehensive. In Exodus 20:10, we have, "But the seventh day is a sabbath to the Lord your God; you shall not do any work—you, your son or your daughter, your male or female slave, your livestock, or the alien resident in your towns." Likewise, Leviticus 25:4–7 states,

> But in the seventh year there shall be a sabbath of complete rest for the land, a sabbath for the Lord: you shall not sow your field or prune your vineyard. You shall not reap the aftergrowth of your harvest or gather the grapes of your unpruned vine: it shall be a year of complete rest for the land. You may eat what the land yields during its sabbath—you, your male and female slaves, your hired and your bound laborers who live with you; for your livestock also, and for the wild animals in your land all its yield shall be for food.

The jubilee provisions, Leviticus 25:11–12, further assert, "That fiftieth year shall be a jubilee for you: you shall not sow, or reap the aftergrowth, or harvest the unpruned vines. For it is a jubilee; it shall be holy to you: you shall eat only what the field itself produces."

As we all know, rest is essential to health and long-term sustainability. But in the trust, rest is not just reserved for humans. It applies to animals and the land itself. The every-seventh-year sabbath for the land is an interesting case. One may wonder if people of that time understood the agricultural benefit of this practice. But allowing a field to rest without cultivation, known as fallowing, improves the tilth (condition) and the fertility of the soil and hence its sustainability. This became a common practice for millennia prior to the use of modern technology and petrochemical fertilizers, herbicides, and pesticides. The soil sustainability benefits of the biblical principle of fallowing are still recognized today, and many organic and sustainable farmers are going back to the practice.

The laws governing jubilee serve another purpose as well, one that harkens back to allotment. As asserted in Leviticus 25:10, 13–17,

> And you shall hallow the fiftieth year and you shall proclaim liberty throughout the land to all its inhabitants. It shall be a jubilee for you: you shall return, every one of you, to your property and every one of you to your family. . . . In this year of jubilee you shall return, every one of you, to your property. When you make a sale to

your neighbor or buy from your neighbor, you shall not cheat one another. When you buy from your neighbor, you shall pay only for the number of years since the jubilee; the seller shall charge you only for the remaining crop years. If the years are more, you shall increase the price, and if the years are fewer, you shall diminish the price; for it is a certain number of harvests that are being sold to you. You shall not cheat one another, but you shall fear your God; for I am the Lord your God.

These provisions recognize and accept that the land will be bought and sold. But every fifty years, people are called to return to their familial inheritance, the land originally allotted to them by God, and sell back any land acquired since the last jubilee at a fair price to the original landholder. There is debate regarding the extent to which the jubilee was actually practiced. Imagine if we tried to implement this practice today. But ultimately, the jubilee is a reminder of who is the true owner of the land. Patrick Miller makes this point:

> Despite the complexities of modern society, the role of land—physical, geographical—is no less important today, for the land functions both as home and as the source of wealth, the means of life. The proper enjoyment of life by all members of the human community depends upon this. A theological understanding of life on the land, however, sets this in a specific context. Although we see the land as bought, worked for, fought for, inherited, we know ultimately that it always comes

to us as God's gift. . . . It comes and will always come not only by human strivings but by the gracious gift of God, who is the true owner of the land and enables us to live on it and use it. . . . Furthermore, human ownership and use of the land are communal as well as individual. While we may and do react at times with renewed assertions of possession and right of ownership, we recognize with Deuteronomy that our life and death on the land are with our neighbor; the inheritance of one is a part of the inheritance of all.[9]

It should be noted that although Miller, here and elsewhere, uses the language of *gift*, what he is describing is not an unconditional giving of the land to any group or individual. Rather, he is describing a relationship wherein God sets conditions, which is much more like a trust. Those conditions are intended to serve the common good, not support the accumulation of human wealth for a select few. This understanding is underscored by Leviticus 25:23: "The land shall not be sold in perpetuity, for the land is mine; with me you are but aliens and tenants." It is also reinforced by Leviticus 19:9–10: "When you reap the harvest of your land, you shall not reap to the very edges of your field, or gather the gleanings of your harvest. You shall not strip your vineyard bare, or gather the fallen grapes of your vineyard; you shall leave them for the poor and the alien: I am the Lord your God." God's desire to have the blessings of the land accessible to all, even the aliens and sojourners among us, is vital to the well-being of human community. This truth is played out in the beautiful saga of Ruth. The action of Ruth, an alien from a foreign land gleaning in Boaz's field, leads to events that sustain and bless many.

Other rules for the trust also pertain to sustainability. They are found in some of the more obscure codes in the Torah, especially in Deuteronomy. Here are some examples:

- Deuteronomy 20:19: "If you besiege a town for a long time, making war against it in order to take it, you must not destroy its trees by wielding an ax against them. Although you may take food from them, you must not cut them down. Are trees in the field human beings that they should come under siege from you?"
- Deuteronomy 22:4: "You shall not see your neighbor's donkey or ox fallen on the road and ignore it; you shall help to lift it up."
- Deuteronomy 22:6–7: "If you come on a bird's nest, in any tree or on the ground, with fledglings or eggs, with the mother sitting on the fledglings or on the eggs, you shall not take the mother with the young. Let the mother go, taking only the young for yourself, in order that it may go well with you and you may live long."
- Deuteronomy 22:10: "You shall not plow with an ox and a donkey yoked together."

It is easy to wonder why these very specific and seemingly insignificant codes have been preserved in the first place. Reading between the lines, there is a principle of sustainability at play in each:

- If you destroy all the fruit trees in war, what happens to the food supply after the war? Many of the major wars in recent centuries resulted in fields not being cultivated and large-scale starvation. Witness Napoleon's scorched-earth policy in retreating from the armies of Russia, or Sherman's March to the Sea during the American Civil War, or the horrible deprivations in Europe after the First and Second World Wars.
- Beasts of burden were part of the agricultural system, and even if they are not yours, they are part of producing and transporting food for the whole community. The welfare of work animals is a communal concern.
- If one eliminates the source of eggs and young, one diminishes the potential for future production and potentially the existence of the species altogether. Think of the number of creatures that have been hunted to extinction or near extinction, such as the American bison and the passenger pigeon.
- Anyone who has worked with draft animals understands that if one mismatches a pair of animals by size and strength, it can result in disabling or killing one or both animals. The stronger animal works too hard, and the weaker animal struggles to keep up.

There is perhaps another principle at work in these obscure texts. It may be that in God's eyes, trees, animals, and birds have inherent worth because God created them, and therefore they should not be subjected to abuse despite the dominion given to human beings. They are to be preserved for the sake of future generations and by virtue of their being created by God.

Consequences of Violating the Trust

A trust has rules, and when there are rules, there are consequences for violating them. When the trust is broken, God sends forth prophets to address the violation and call for a restoration of justice and righteousness. There are many instances recorded in the Old Testament of prophets speaking out against those who break the codes and laws pertaining to the care and sustaining of God's people and the rest of God's creation:

> Ah, you who join house to house, who add field to field, until there is room for no one but you, and you are left to live alone in the midst of the land! The Lord of hosts has sworn in my hearing: Surely many houses shall be desolate, large and beautiful houses, without inhabitant. For ten acres of vineyard shall yield but one bath, and a homer of seed shall yield a mere ephah. (Isa 5:8–10)

> Ah, you that turn justice to wormwood, and bring righteousness to the ground! . . . They hate the one who reproves in the gate, and they abhor the one who speaks the truth. Therefore because you trample on the poor and take from them levies of grain, you have built houses of hewn stone, but you shall not live in them; you have planted pleasant vineyards, but you shall not drink their wine. (Amos 5:7, 10–11)

Alas for those who devise wickedness and evil deeds on their beds! When the morning dawns, they perform it, because it is in their power. They covet fields, and seize them; houses, and take them away; they oppress householder and house, people and their inheritance. Therefore thus says the Lord: Now, I am devising against this family an evil from which you cannot remove your necks; and you shall not walk haughtily, for it will be an evil time. (Mic 2:1–3)

Isaiah, Amos, and Micah are called to confront rich and powerful people who are abusing common folk—taxing them unjustly, taking their land and homes, and displacing them. The impact on the victims of these violations was dire. Farmers were compelled to produce export crops for the profit of the rich who now controlled the land. As a result, those farming the land found themselves at an extreme disadvantage and sometimes were forced into poverty and hunger. The prophets spoke out against such violations boldly and clearly.

Numerous modern scholars have focused on these passages in their historic context. Their analyses highlight the text's remarkably contemporary ring. Ellen F. Davis observes,

The old subsistence economy . . . was supplanted by intensified and specialized agriculture. The new system was designed to maximize production of the three most important commodities: grain to feed the cities . . . and wine and olive oil, the more expensive products, to provide export revenue and to satisfy . . . the taste for

luxury now cultivated among the few who were rich. . . .
Altogether, the demands of the centralized government
may well have consumed half or more of a family's labor
and production capacity. In a bad agricultural year . . .
many families would have been unable to feed themselves
and also meet the demands of the state. So the crown literally gained ground for centralized agriculture through
acquisition of the ancestral lands of small farmers who
went into debt and put up their land as collateral.[10]

And James Luther Mays, in reference to Micah, states, "The old
family properties around the villages were being broken up and
the clan system pressed out of existence. Micah, whose home was
in one of the villages, must have known through bitter experience
the anguish and humiliation of this economic progress. But he
also knows that both motive and deed of those who prospered
thereby was a violation of YHWH's will and would bring divine
punishment upon them."[11] The commercialization, commodifi-
cation, and consolidation of landholdings and the subsequent
impact on farmers are as real today as they were in the time of
the prophets.

There is also narrative material within the historical books
of the Old Testament that addresses the consequences of violating the trust. One prime example is the fascinating story
of Naboth's vineyard in 1 Kings, which encapsulates many of
the prophets' proclamations regarding proper relationship to the
land and one's neighbor. Naboth, a common citizen, had an
orchard next to King Ahab's palace in Jezreel. Ahab thinks it

would be most convenient if he owned that vineyard so he could plant a vegetable garden there. The king offers to purchase the land outright or trade for a better vineyard, but Naboth refuses, saying, "The Lord forbid that I should give you my ancestral inheritance" (1 Kgs 21:3). Ahab pouts. Then Queen Jezebel tells him that he is the ruler of Israel; he can have that land if he so chooses. She devises a plan whereby Naboth is wrongly accused of blasphemy and is stoned to death. With Naboth dead, Ahab takes possession of the vineyard. Then the Lord sends Elijah with a dire prophecy: "Thus says the Lord: Have you killed, and also taken possession? . . . Thus says the Lord: In the place where dogs licked up the blood of Naboth, dogs will also lick up your blood" (1 Kgs 21:19). This divination is eventually fulfilled in 1 Kings 22:34–38. Of course, this event involves Ahab's breaking at least four of the Ten Commandments: (1) you shall not murder, (2) you shall not steal, (3) you shall not bear false witness, and (4) you shall not covet. But Naboth's refusal also hearkens back to the original allotment of the land and God's ultimate claim on the land, as well God's desire that justice be carried out in relationship to the land. God forbid that Naboth should give away his ancestral inheritance. Ahab and Jezebel use power and deceit to take it and suffer the consequences.

Another consequence of violating the trust is often referred to as the "curse of futility." When the trust is violated, the creation itself responds. We've had one example already in Isaiah 5:10: "For ten acres of vineyard shall yield but one bath, and a homer of seed shall yield a mere ephah." Another example is found in Leviticus 20:22: "You shall keep all my statutes and all my ordinances, and observe them, so that the land to which I bring you to settle in may not vomit you out." Perhaps the most extensive treatments of the consequences for violating the land are the blessings and curses found in Deuteronomy 28. The curses, verses 15–46, are gruesome as they relate to the people, but it is significant how many of them relate to the creation, its creatures, and agriculture. Land and fields, livestock and seed, vineyards and orchards—all will be cursed "because you did not serve the Lord your God joyfully and with gladness of heart for the abundance of everything" (Deut 28:47). All of creation suffers because of humanity's lack of grateful obedience in response to the abundant blessings of God's creation.

Restoration of the Trust

Though the consequences for violating the trust are dire, there is hope for restoration. There is a way back:

> If you follow my statutes and keep my commandments and observe them faithfully, I will give you your rains in their season, and the land shall yield its produce, and the trees of the field shall yield their fruit. Your threshing shall overtake the vintage, and the vintage shall overtake the sowing; you shall eat your bread to the full, and live securely in your land. (Lev 26:3–5)

> Return to the Lord, your God, for he is gracious and merciful, slow to anger, and abounding in steadfast love, and relents from punishing. (Joel 2:13)

He has told you, O mortal, what is good; and what does
the Lord require of you but to do justice, and to love
kindness, and to walk humbly with your God? (Mic 6:8)

God does not give up on what God has created. It is the creator's
desire that all be redeemed and restored.

In Jeremiah, we hear of God's promise of redemption and
restoration, symbolized by the purchase of a family farm field during the Babylonian siege of Jerusalem. In chapter 32, God speaks
to Jeremiah, who is under house arrest in the palace in Jerusalem,
and tells him to buy a field at Anathoth from his cousin Hanamel.
Anathoth was Jeremiah's hometown, not far from the walls of
Jerusalem. To buy the field would keep it in the family. Jeremiah
complies, and there is a lengthy description of this agricultural land
transaction. From a strictly business perspective, this would appear
to be a very bad deal. Who would invest in land that is about to be
overrun by a powerful enemy? But God has in mind that this mundane act will be a sign of hope: "For thus says the Lord of hosts,
the God of Israel: Houses and fields and vineyards shall again be
bought in this land" (Jer 32:15). Gunther H. Wittenberg observes,
"Only in the harmony of houses, fields and vineyards, in mutual
interdependence is new life assured. . . . Fields and vineyards, in
short the land, have their intrinsic worth. The land gives new life to
wholeness and healing. But just as the land becomes the custodian
of the new life, the families need to be the custodians of the land.
A central element of this vision is mutual custodianship."[12]

The importance of this relationship between land and people
outweighs any financial considerations. Wittenberg continues,

Land, in this view, has intrinsic worth. It has to be kept in the possession of the family, and to be redeemed from unscrupulous speculators, even if this redemption does not bring direct financial benefits. . . . Only through a new vision of land, which rediscovers its intrinsic worth, so central in the ancient Israelite view that we also find in Jeremiah, and the close bond between people and land, can a new sense of custodianship be developed, which treats the land not as dead material for personal gain, but as the living Earth which needs to be nurtured and preserved for future generations.[13]

God promises that a right relationship between land and people, creation and community will be restored. And hence we come to our creator God's new thing: the savior and redeemer Jesus Christ.

A Potluck of New Testament Connections

The New Testament narrative seems less concerned about the issues of food and sustainability than does the Old Testament. This is largely due to the eschatological urgency present in the early church, the expectation that Christ was coming again soon. There was no need to dwell on long-term, multigenerational questions about the land and creation. The early disciples of Christ were anxiously awaiting a new creation, a new heaven and a new earth. But still the call for justice for all that God has made can be clearly heard.

First, we need to affirm that Jesus, the man, was shaped by a rural agrarian context. Born in Bethlehem and raised in Nazareth, he and his family were surrounded by fields and flocks. Jesus drew on this context for many of his parables—planting and harvest, seeds and weeds, sheep and shepherds, nets and fish—the mundane daily realities of producing food and fiber. Jesus understood the land and the people of the land. But we must also recognize that Jesus's miracles demonstrate his divinity. Many exhibit his power over creation, including stilling the storm (Matt 8:23–27; Mark 4:36–41; Luke 8:23–25) and walking on water (Matt 14:22–33; Mark 6:45–52). In the stilling of the storm, the disciples question Jesus's true identity: "Who then is this, that even the wind and the sea obey him?" (Mark 4:41). In Matthew's account, after Jesus walks on water and enters the boat, the disciples worship him (Matt 14:33). Worship is reserved for the divine. The prologue of John is even more direct in relating Jesus to the creator: "In the beginning was the Word, and the Word was with God, and the Word was God. He was in the beginning with God. All things came into being through him, and without him not one thing came into being. What has come into being in him was life, and the life was the light of all people. The light shines in the darkness, and the darkness did not overcome it" (John 1:1–5).

Though writing metaphorically, it is clear that the evangelist envisions Jesus as codivine cocreator from the beginning. Christ Jesus, Son of God, bears the same claim on creation, the same authority over creation, and the same desire for sustaining justice for the creation as does the creator God, because, as Jesus says, "The Father and I are one" (John 10:30). Jesus, fully human, is an ancient Near Eastern rural carpenter from Galilee shaped by the earthy realities of that context. Jesus, fully divine, is God.

One miracle, the Feeding of the Five Thousand, demonstrates more than Jesus's divinity. Obviously, this miracle, the only one recorded in some form by all four evangelists, was considered particularly important by the early church. It is profound on a variety of levels. Let us focus on Matthew's version:

> When it was evening, the disciples came to him [Jesus] and said, "This is a deserted place, and the hour is now late; send the crowds away so that they may go into the villages and buy food for themselves." Jesus said to them, "They need not go away; you give them something to eat." They replied, "We have nothing here but five loaves and two fish." And he said, "Bring them here to me." Then he ordered the crowds to sit down on the grass. Taking the five loaves and the two fish, he looked up to heaven, and blessed and broke the loaves, and gave them to the disciples, and the disciples gave them to the crowds. And all ate and were filled; and they took up what was left over of the broken pieces, twelve baskets full. And those who ate were about five thousand men, besides women and children. (Matt 14:15–21)

While dealing with the news that John the Baptist had been executed, Jesus seeks some time alone. But he is beset by a great crowd of people with needs. Jesus graciously meets those needs and heals their sick. Despite witnessing their teacher's miraculous abundance of compassion, when the sun goes down, the disciples can see only scarcity. Jesus then proceeds to demonstrate the power of God's abundance. They do not need to succumb to the fear of scarcity, for with God, there is enough—more than enough. When one views life from the perspective of plenty, one can truly "serve the Lord your God joyfully and with gladness of heart for the abundance of everything" (Deut 28:47). As a result, everyone gets to eat.

Jesus, as the Son of God, asserts his authority in relationship to rules of the creation trust discussed earlier in this chapter. In the Gospel of Mark, Jesus is confronted by a group of Pharisees and makes an argument for a liberal interpretation of the rules of the sabbath:

> One sabbath he [Jesus] was going through the grainfields; and as they made their way his disciples began to pluck heads of grain. The Pharisees said to him, "Look, why are they doing what is not lawful on the sabbath?" And he said to them, "Have you never read what David did when he and his companions were hungry and in need of food? He entered the house of God, when Abiathar was high priest, and ate the bread of the Presence, which it is not lawful for any but the priests to eat, and he gave some to his companions." Then he said to them, "The sabbath was made for humankind, and not humankind for the sabbath; so the Son of Man is lord even of the sabbath." (Mark 2:23–28)

On the surface, this is another of Jesus's debates with the Pharisees over the interpretation of the law and another of their attempts to trip up Jesus on some sort of technical violation. But in the background of this confrontation are some of the rules of the trust we discussed earlier. There is the command to leave some crop in the field for the sake of those who need it, including hungry travelers passing through, as in Leviticus 19:9. Thus the issue was not whether it was permitted to take the grain in the first place; the issue was when the disciples took it—on the sabbath. Jesus's rejoinder, supported with a reference from Scripture, is pointed and revealing. Jesus applies a broad interpretation of the intent of the sabbath, stressing God's desire that the blessings of God's creation be available to all. That principle supersedes a narrow understanding circumscribed by a particular day of the week: "The sabbath was made for humankind, and not humankind for the sabbath." But then Jesus asserts his authority to make such an interpretation. This is bold indeed. The sabbath was ordained by God's command. To claim lordship over the sabbath is to put himself on equal footing with God. Part of Jesus's lordship is to enforce justice for humanity and for all creation.

In Matthew, the last major teaching of Jesus prior to his death and resurrection speaks to the final judgment. It is in the form of curse and blessing. The following is the blessing side of the judgment:

> Then the king will say to those at his right hand, "Come, you that are blessed by my Father, inherit the kingdom prepared for you from the foundation of the world; for I was hungry and you gave me food, I was thirsty and you gave me something to drink, I was a stranger and you welcomed me, I was naked and you gave me clothing, I was sick and you took care of me, I was in prison and you visited me." Then the righteous will answer him,

"Lord, when was it that we saw you hungry and gave you food, or thirsty and gave you something to drink? And when was it that we saw you a stranger and welcomed you, or naked and gave you clothing? And when was it that we saw you sick or in prison and visited you?" And the king will answer them, "Truly I tell you, just as you did it to one of the least of these who are members of my family, you did it to me." (Matt 25:34–40)

Once again, Jesus stresses God's desire that all should be blessed from the abundance of God's provision. In the spirit of Micah 6:8, the call to live righteously is based on simple and practical kindness, justice, and humbleness: food for the hungry, drink for the thirsty, provisions for the poor and needy, kindness and hospitality for the stranger, alien, and marginalized. Elaine M. Wainwright argues that this eschatological ethic can or perhaps should be applied to the whole of creation: "They [the righteous] re-order or order in right relationship . . . not just the human but the other-than-human and the interrelationship of the two."[14] Furthermore, "this is an ethic for the now of the Matthean community and for the now of communities today. It is an ethic that can catch up the human and other-than-human in a re-ordering of right relationships. If . . . such a right ordering . . . were to be taken in today's human communities in their relationships with all in the other-than-human communities around planet Earth, this would truly manifest the *basileia* [dominion, rule] of the heavens."[15]

This reading of the interconnectedness of human and non-human creation resonates with Paul's reflections in the Letter

to the Romans. In Romans 8, the apostle Paul seems to be applying the curse of futility as he speaks of creation's anticipation
of the fullness of redemption promised in Jesus Christ:

> I consider that the sufferings of this present time are not
> worth comparing with the glory about to be revealed to us.
> For the creation waits with eager longing for the revealing
> of the children of God; for the creation was subjected to
> futility, not of its own will but by the will of the one who
> subjected it, in hope that the creation itself will be set free
> from its bondage to decay and will obtain the freedom of
> the glory of the children of God. We know that the whole
> creation has been groaning in labor pains until now; and
> not only the creation, but we ourselves, who have the first
> fruits of the Spirit, groan inwardly while we wait for adop-
> tion, the redemption of our bodies. For in hope we were
> saved. Now hope that is seen is not hope. For who hopes
> for what is seen? But if we hope for what we do not see,
> we wait for it with patience. (Rom 8:18–25)

It is not just humankind that has been waiting; the whole of creation has a stake in God's ultimate act of redemption and salvation
and the coming of a new heaven and a new earth. Humanity's violations of God's covenant and the rules of the creation trust have
impacted creation itself with futility and bondage to decay. The
posterity of humankind and the rest of creation are intertwined.
Sigve Tonstad writes, "If we still wonder why Paul brings up the
subject of non-human creation, the best answer is that Paul was not
the kind of thinker tradition made him out to be. His widescreen

gospel is bigger, more earthy, and far more inclusive. In all and for all, including non-human reality, hope is ascendant. The night of plight is receding before the light of revelation of the faithfulness of God. In this hope the entire non-human creation 'has been groaning in labor pains until now.'"[16]

And so there is hope for the future. A vision of this restoration comes in the revelation of John: "Then the angel showed me the river of the water of life, bright as crystal, flowing from the throne of God and of the Lamb through the middle of the street of the city. On either side of the river is the tree of life with its twelve kinds of fruit, producing its fruit each month; and the leaves of the tree are for the healing of the nations" (Rev 22:1–2). The imagery of the closing of John's vision creates a poetic book-end to the whole of Scripture, reversing the curse brought on by the original transgression as recorded in Genesis 3. Humanity was expelled from the garden of Eden and barred from the tree of life, and the ground itself was cursed. In the new heaven and the new earth, all that is undone. And on occasion, we are given a glimpse of this in the present earth.

In the mid-1980s, my spouse and I served as short-term lay missionary teachers in Hong Kong for the American Lutheran Church. We taught English language, world history, and Bible knowledge at a Chinese Lutheran Middle School. Those three years were eye opening and life changing for us. But one day has deeply affected me in the thirty-five years since and reoriented my understanding of abundance and hospitality. We were there amid the height of the influx of Vietnamese refugees known as boat people. Tens of thousands of refugees were held in camps in the

British colony. Our Lutheran mission assisted the Red Cross in managing one of the camps, Kai Tak North. The Lutheran Church ran a school for children in the camp as well as adult language classes and vocational retraining in anticipation of resettlement. One day, we visited the camp. The refugees were housed in large Quonset buildings that were lined with three-tiered bunk beds made of four-by-eight plywood with thin foam mattresses. A family might have three beds, an individual just one. There was virtually no personal space. (We recognized the handmade quilts that had been donated to Lutheran World Relief by groups in the United States were being used to provide warmth and walls for some privacy.) There were communal fires outside the buildings to heat water for washing and for tea.

One of our Lutheran missionaries who served as the principal of the school gave us a tour. Eventually, we were greeted by an older woman who spoke Cantonese, which our guide could translate. She had escaped with part of her family. Her grandkids were in school, and the other adults were in language class. She told us her story and showed us her home, a three-tiered bunk with the family's clothes in neatly folded piles on the beds. They had a small side table and a couple of footlockers. At one point, she indicated that she wanted to serve us tea and biscuits. I balked. I felt I didn't want to deprive her of what little she had. Our colleague told us that to refuse her hospitality would be an insult; besides, she said she was grateful. "Grateful?" I asked. "Yes, grateful for the people who have helped them and grateful for the opportunity for a new life," was the response. The woman opened one of the footlockers and took out a small tin of tea, a small tin of biscuits, and what seemed to be a child's tea set. She gave us each a biscuit, carefully measured out tea leaves into the pot, and went to the fire for hot water. She served us tea, and we feasted. I was humbled. All I had seen was scarcity; she saw abundance so that her guests would eat that afternoon, even if it was just a biscuit and a small cup of tea.

In the intervening years, as I have lived with and studied in more depth many of the Scripture passages presented in this chapter, I have frequently recalled this chance encounter. I have reflected on the fact that we were both sojourners and aliens in a foreign land, dependent on the kindness and hospitality of others—food given to the hungry, a hospitality to which God's word calls us. This elderly Vietnamese woman taught me a profound lesson about the abundance of God's creation and God's grace. I hear Jesus's command to his disciples: "They need not go away; you give them something to eat." I hear God calling to "serve the Lord your God joyfully and with gladness of heart for the abundance of everything." There is enough. Through the law and the prophets, God calls us to share the bounty of creation and work to sustain the creation that produces our daily bread. Everyone is to benefit from what God provides. Everyone must eat.

I close this chapter with a challenge from James Limburg: "In this time of ecological urgency, the considerable collection of biblical texts dealing with earth care ought not to be confined to consideration in academies or learned journals. These texts need to be studied, given a fresh hearing, and then set loose in the world. Rightly understood, they can light some fires, ignite some concern and indicate a direction for our communities, our churches, and our synagogues."[17] This directive is as relevant today as when it was penned a quarter of a century ago. It is a challenge that needs to be taken up by those of us on the front lines of mission and ministry.

Questions for Reflection and Discussion

1. Of the many Scripture passages addressed in this chapter, which are the most striking or captivating to you? Which are the most challenging? In what way?

2. Are there passages that you think are missing from the menu? If so, what are they? How do they speak to the issues of food and sustainability?

3. How are you as an individual fulfilling the trust? In what ways are you violating the trust? How about your congregation or parish?

4. As a society, in what ways are we in compliance with or in violation of the trust?

5. Where we are in violation, what are some ways we can act to restore the trust?

4

Incarnating Hope

The Art of Leadership for Christian Ministry in a Hungry World

The 2017 feature film *All Saints* tells the true story of the people of All Saints, a small Episcopalian congregation in Smyrna, Tennessee, and a group of Karen (pronounced Kah-REN) refugees (from Burma/Myanmar) who found each other. Both groups were struggling in their own ways. The Karen, displaced by war, came to Tennessee with virtually nothing. They were going to bed hungry. All Saints was losing members and was struggling to survive financially. They had been scheduled for closure by their diocese. But they had farmable land, and their new neighbors knew how to farm. They listened to each other and built a shared story rooted in God. Faith, the need to eat, and good land entrusted to a small, struggling Episcopalian congregation brought two diverse groups together. And now in that faith community, no one goes to bed hungry. God did a new thing, and both groups found new life. "It was kind of a miracle," said Michael Spurlock, who was pastor of All Saints at the time. "God had sent more than 70 expert farmers to the church at the hour of their greatest need."[1]

I have witnessed a very similar story play out in a tiny town in southwestern Minnesota, in a small congregation now called the Asian American Christian Reformed Church of Bigelow (AACRC). The congregation didn't always have *Asian American* in its name. In the 1980s and early '90s, the congregation was shrinking along with the town. A few families connected to the Dutch Reformed heritage of the congregation continued its mission and ministry but were questioning their long-term sustainability. About that time, the large pork processing plant in nearby Worthington, Minnesota, reduced its wages and increased the speed of its processing lines to increase productivity and profitability. Consequently, the plant lost a significant proportion of its primarily Caucasian workers who didn't want to work under those circumstances.

The company began recruiting Hispanic Americans from the southern United States and new immigrants to fill these jobs. As these people resettled in the Worthington area, many sought more affordable housing in the smaller satellite towns like Bigelow. One early summer during those years, the organizers of the Vacation Bible School for the Christian Reformed Church (CRC) decided to visit every home in their town and, if the household had children, invite them to Vacation Bible School (VBS). In that process, the members of the CRC were surprised by how many homes were now occupied by Asian— Vietnamese and Laotian—families with young children, who lived quietly in the community and worked, went to school, and shopped in Worthington. These families were invited to VBS, like everyone else in town, and several of those Asian households sent their children. And these families continued to come to worship. The younger people and some adults could speak English. The congregation engaged in social ministry, helping their new neighbors and members negotiate social services, such as school communications and medical needs. The pastor, Ron Lammers, learned Lao. The congregation trained some key leaders in the Vietnamese and Laotian community to be evangelists and teachers. Worship attendance and especially Sunday school was revitalized. But financial challenges remained.

For a while, the Christian Reformed denomination took on the Bigelow congregation as a mission development. This eased some of the financial concerns. But eventually, the denomination demanded that the congregation move into the city of Worthington. There was disagreement within the congregation as to whether this would be wise, and members held a congregational vote. The longer-term Asian members had developed an attachment to the simple wooden church building, in part because the architecture vaguely resembled houses of worship in their homeland. The congregation split, some voting to move and some to stay. Part of the congregation relocated to Worthington and was led by one of the trained evangelists. The rest stayed in Bigelow, and Rev. Lammers stayed with them. The denomination cut mission support to the Bigelow contingent. Yet the congregation still serves. I worship with them once or twice a year when I am in that area. The worship is in at least three languages—like a mini Pentecost. The Sunday school is alive again. The potlucks are amazing cross-cultural experiences.

Recently, a Guatemalan Evangelical congregation, which had been gathering in an empty storefront in Worthington, heard about the hospitality of the AACRC and asked if they could worship there on Sunday afternoon and share expenses for the building. So now as the Asian American potluck is winding down in the basement, the horns, accordions, guitars, and drums of the Guatemalan worship band is firing up in the sanctuary upstairs. There you will hear Spanish and Guatemalan Indigenous dialects and witness standing room only, with the center aisle lined with baby carriers.

The globalized food system brought people from many places in the world to southwestern Minnesota. By welcoming and partnering with their new neighbors, a small rural congregation found a new reason to be. Faith, food, and music bridge the differences they have, and God is doing a new thing.

I share these stories for a number of reasons. First, they are very real stories about the interconnections of food, justice, and ministry—globally and locally. In addition, they demonstrate some of the skills involved in the art of ministering in a hungry world, skills we will explore shortly. Finally, when faced with the complex challenges of food justice and sustainability, it is easy to descend into pessimism. Stories like these inspire hope and lift up what is possible. Hope is a vital component of faith and ministry and an incentive to tackle difficult challenges. As the apostle Paul proclaims, "Therefore, since we are justified by faith, we have peace with God through our Lord Jesus Christ, through whom we have obtained access to this grace in which we stand; and we boast in our hope of sharing the glory of God. And not only that, but we also boast in our sufferings, knowing that suffering produces endurance, and endurance produces character, and character produces hope, and hope does not disappoint us, because God's love has been poured into our hearts through the Holy Spirit that has been given to us" (Rom 5:1–5).

Brueggemann expresses the importance of hope in this way: "The urging to bring hope to public expression is based on a conviction about believing folks. It is premised on the capacity to evoke and bring to expression the hope that is within us. It is there within and among us, for we are ordained of God to be people of hope."[2] Hope is a key ingredient of the art of leadership for Christian ministry in a hungry world. A good leader embodies hope. Hope is the energy that empowers people to persevere as well as take on God's challenge to do justice, love kindness, and walk humbly with their God.

Along with hope, the Christian leader must make artful use of the prophetic office to lead and minister in a hungry world. Often, *prophetic* is understood as a matter of predicting the future. But I believe the prophetic office is about seeing and interpreting how God is at work in the present. Amid challenge and change, it is difficult to see let alone perceive what God is doing. God's people need leaders with open eyes and open ears so that, to the best of their human ability, such leaders can perceive, understand, and then point out to God's people the ways God is present and at work among them. This need is especially acute in rural communities. Leaders need to be bold and declare, "Behold, God is still here!" and proclaim in the words of the beloved hymn "This Is My Father's World," "And though the wrong seems oft so strong, God is the ruler yet." In that there is hope.

Skillful use of story is also a vital component of this art of ministering in a hungry world. Thomas Groome, in his book *Sharing Faith: A Comprehensive Approach to Religious Education and Pastoral Ministry, the Way of Shared Praxis*, describes a pedagogical method he calls shared praxis. Rather than a teacher dispensing information to learners as if they are empty vessels, the teacher, according to this principle, recognizes that everyone brings something to the learning event. Everyone has experience, a story. The goal is to weave together your story (one's personal narrative) with their story (another's narrative) with God's story (the biblical narrative) to create our story (a communal narrative). Such praxis involves skillful and faithful listening—creating an environment where people feel safe to share their stories. The method requires the integration of individuals' stories with theological reflection—the thoughtful consideration of how the biblical narrative informs and shapes our individual narratives. Finally, there is discernment, by the participants led by the facilitator/teacher, of how participants might have been influenced or changed by this shared praxis process. Participants also explore how they might be different as a group, a community. Often, this process results in changed attitudes or perspectives, and it sometimes produces changed behaviors or stimulates new actions by individuals or groups. Groome calls this final step "making decisions or responses for lived Christian life."[3]

Although Groome's work initially focused on religious education, he has also applied the method to other facets of ministry—preaching, worship, counseling, and peace and justice ministry, the last encompassing issues of food justice and sustainability. Tex Sample, in *Ministry in an Oral Culture*, also speaks to the application of narrative to justice issues.[4]

Let me offer an example of how this works from my own experience. A care-of-creation conference was held at Shalom Hill Farm (SHF), and the focus was on trees and their importance in the environment locally and globally. Participants were clergy and lay church members from various places, and some of them included farmers and individuals who worked for government soil and water conservation agencies. A naturalist and a soil conservation expert presented. My role was to relate the biblical narrative to the topic. In my session, I began by asking each of the conference participants to tell a story about how trees were important to them. There were personal stories about a favorite tree to climb in childhood. There were stories about planting trees in groves and windbreaks and stories of pruning and picking fruit. There were stories of trees that had fallen or blown over and created problems and even personal trauma. We then looked at various biblical texts that featured trees and focused on one in particular: "If you besiege a town for a long time, making war against it in order to take it, you must not destroy its trees by wielding an ax against them. Although you may take food from them, you must not cut them down. Are trees in the field human beings that they should come under siege from you? You may destroy only the trees that you know do not produce food; you may cut them down for use in building siegeworks against the town that makes war with you, until it falls" (Deut 20:19–20).

I asked, "Why do you think this very specific command from God about trees is included in Scripture?" Responses generally fell into two categories: that God inherently cares about trees, especially those that produce fruit, and that this is an issue of sustainability. Even in war, there should be a concern for the ongoing sustainability of the environment and future communities. We concluded with some discussion about what all this might mean concerning our individual and communal relationship to trees.

After the session, I noticed that two of the participants were off in a corner having a very animated conversation. One was a local farmer, and one was a local federal conservation official. I knew them both from different contexts. Later I asked the conservation official what their discussion was about. He said the two of them had been in a long-standing conflict over preserving several tree windbreaks protecting soil from wind erosion in some large farm fields in the area. The farmer had bought several additional acres of land from neighbors who had quit farming. With more land, the farmer needed to use larger machinery, and he wanted to take all the windbreaks down because they were a hindrance to his equipment. The official was trying to prevent him from destroying the trees because they had been planted for soil conservation and funded in part by federal dollars. Apparently, this issue had become so heated, it had nearly ended up in court. But the official said they just had the most amiable and fruitful conversation about their conflict after that Bible study. Eventually, the two reached a compromise: some of the trees were removed to allow passage from field to field with the equipment, and the others were preserved. Those trees are still in place today.

I have used this method in preaching, visitation, and Bible study and in leading groups in visioning for the future. Thomas Groome's method is effective because the process honors narrative—people's experience and knowledge—while giving due credence to the biblical narrative together with more empirical sources, such as science. It functions well in a variety of contexts but especially in small-town and rural settings, where story is a significant part of the culture. As we reflect on how our mission and ministry, individually and congregationally, address the reality that everyone must eat and that we are called to be co-stewards with God in maintaining the ongoing sustainability of creation, this method of narrative-based theological reflection can be an excellent tool to guide our discussions.

Tending to the Creation in Your Backyard

There is probably little any one of us can do individually about food and sustainability that would have an impact on a global scale. But in keeping with the slogan "Think globally, act locally," there are things we can do locally that make a difference, and the cumulative effect can be significant. That is, in essence, what happened at All Saints in Tennessee and the AACRC in Minnesota. They found themselves drawn into the global refugee crisis. At All Saints, the Karen people needed a place to grow food. At the AACRC, their new neighbors needed help navigating the realities of their new home. Despite speaking different languages, these people managed to listen to each other and build a shared story rooted in God. Now those little congregations in those small towns are filled with people who sing with new life in many different languages.

In truth, all of us, regardless of community context, have been given a place, a space, in creation for which to care. It may be in a city or in the countryside. It probably is not the size of a ranch or a farm. It may be a yard, a garden, or a flower box. It could be the grounds of a business, a local park, a school, or a church. It could be the people and places of our community. The point is that we as people of faith need to recognize and continually remind ourselves that we do not exist in isolation from the rest of God's creation. We are part of it. And we have been uniquely tasked to be co-stewards of the creation with the creator. That task is not about seemingly insurmountable problems in faraway places. It starts at home, in our backyards. The aforementioned Dr. William Heffernan was at SHF leading a conference on the global food system with all its complexities. SHF had a policy to try to incorporate as many locally produced ingredients as possible in our meals. At one meal, Dr. Heffernan caught me apologizing for the fact that we had only three locally produced foods on the menu. He took me aside and told me never to apologize. He said, "You are never going to change the global food system. But you can do this. Every time you make a conscious decision to serve even one locally produced food, and you share that with your guests, you have made a difference." Here are some ways in which congregations and individuals are making a difference.

There has been a movement in the United States over the past thirty years to establish creation-awareness congregations. This movement has a global reach as well, finding expression in numerous Western countries. The basic premise is that a congregation can do a lot to make their space more creation friendly as well as to raise awareness among its members about the larger national and global issues. In numerous locales, clusters of congregations work together on care-of-creation issues for their congregations and communities. And of course, the more congregations that make this effort, the larger the impact. Most denominations have created networks and websites to equip and encourage congregations in this endeavor. One of my favorites is an ecumenical organization rooted in the Church of England and based in Britain called Operation Noah (https://operationnoah .org). Their tagline is "Faith-Motivated. Science-Informed. Hope-Inspired." Their website has numerous engaging resources in a variety of media. Most of the websites for these various faith-based associations are a treasure trove of resources and ideas.

Congregations that choose to participate in the creation-awareness movement need to be prepared for "kitchen wars," the term I use to describe debates about seemingly small, mundane things that become big issues in some people's minds. Questions like whether to serve fair-trade or organic beverages, use real dishes or Styrofoam and paper, or make the building energy efficient, to name just a few common issues, can become bones of contention, especially when short-term costs and time are considered. Responding to the old joke "How many parishioners does it take to change a light bulb?" a Presbyterian colleague said,

"Twelve—one to hold the light bulb, four to turn the step ladder, and seven to form a committee to debate the wattage of the bulb." But networking with other congregations and organizations with shared care and concern can cross-pollinate ideas, energize local efforts, and buoy the spirits of those who, at times, may feel as though they are pushing a boulder up a hill.

In addition to their building facilities, most congregations own some land—either a couple of acres or a congregationally managed cemetery. Some congregations even own farmland that has been donated. I am aware of a congregation that owns and manages a forty-acre stand of timber. Developing an imagination for what can be done outside the building, depending on the climate, creates opportunities to make a difference locally. As with the aforementioned decisions about what food is served and how it is served in a church building, a primary challenge is to be intentional about land management practices. For example, a significant amount of fertilizer runoff comes from urban lawns. Fertilizer creates algae blooms in surface water and can leach into groundwater. In some watersheds, more fertilizer runs off from urban landscapes than from agricultural sources. Often, lawn fertilizer is overapplied, whereas the application of agricultural fertilizers is regulated and monitored with technology, so only the amount needed is applied, meaning it is far less likely to result in water contamination. Proper application ensures that fertilizer is retained in the soil and consumed by the plants for which it is intended and does not enter local water sources. Being intentional about what type and how much fertilizer is applied to a churchyard, if at all, is one small but significant way to help improve water quality.

Another step is to consider whether all landscaping needs to be decorative. Some congregations dedicate land to community gardens. All Saints created a small truck farm to grow Asian vegetables for the Karen's consumption and for sale in local farmers' markets. Some congregations plant edible landscape—vegetables and vining fruits that can be harvested and sold or donated to a food shelf. Such creative ideas can help educate people, especially the younger generations, about where food comes from and how to grow it. In many places, gardening and cooking with fresh ingredients is a dying art. A fun project for youth is a pizza garden—growing the ingredients and then making pizza from scratch and enjoying the healthy and flavorful experience of eating homegrown, homemade food. Such projects make great intergenerational opportunities, and even a failed or partially failed crop is a learning experience, a microcosm of the challenges production farmers face.

Even on a small scale, converting church grounds to food production sites requires a balance of aesthetic sensitivity and practicality. And these endeavors require committed people to carry them out. There will be disagreements. Like kitchen wars, issues of grass and gardens can grow into turf wars. I would recommend working with congregational leaders to establish policies for the interior and the exterior of the church facilities, based on a consensus of congregational members, that grow out of the mission of the congregation and make creation care a priority. This helps raise awareness that part of what we do as people of faith is account for God's creation in our decision-making. Those decisions should not be governed by purely economic or aesthetic considerations.

Many if not most church-related camps have care-of-creation programming and are wonderful models of how this can be done. Camps have large physical footprints that require substantial effort to maintain them faithfully and sustainably. Holden Village (http:// www.holdenvillage.org), a Lutheran ministry in Washington State, is a prime example. In 1960, Holden Village was established in a former mining town of the same name that had closed in 1957. Sustaining creation justice is written into its core values and lived out in the day-to-day experience of the community. In their time at the camp, guests learn about and live in a way that leaves a lighter footprint upon the land. Sustainable management is practiced in a variety of ways, small and large. Guests learn the benefits and importance of composting, waste reduction, local food production, and water conservation. Beginning in 2013, Holden Village engaged in a major, public-private, cooperative endeavor to redeem the land in their midst from the toxic impact of past mining. The recovery work involved cleaning up mining tailings and building a new water treatment facility.

Another surprising and terrific example is Pilgrim Place (https://www.pilgrimplace.org), a faith-based senior living community dedicated to peace and justice based in Claremont, California. Creation care is part of the community ethos. Collectively, the community has reduced its water consumption by 50 percent since 2000. They actively seek ways to reduce their carbon footprint, including the installation of over two thousand solar panels. A group of residents raise organic fruit and vegetables for consumption in the community or to sell to raise money for the Residents' Health and Support fund.

Some congregations build coalitions between food growers and food consumers. They connect the congregation with existing community-supported agriculture (CSA) organizations or establish what some call congregationally supported agriculture, the other CSA. As a result, farmers receive more of the food dollar, consumers get fresh food and know what is in it, and farmers and consumers can build relationship. In one suburban setting, a Roman Catholic congregation and a Lutheran congregation share a large parking lot. On Saturdays in the summer, that parking lot becomes a wonderful farmer's market, a multigenerational, ecumenical setting for food, crafts, and fun. Some congregations have established relationships across rural/urban divides. They have done pulpit exchanges and congregational visits, establishing cross-cultural learning opportunities. Occasionally, these efforts develop into direct marketing networks. In one such congregational network, called Holy Cows, beef farmers sell a share in a cow (one-eighth up to a whole animal), raise it, have it processed, and deliver it to their city brothers and sisters. Some great relationships have been built because of this network. Of course, there are also the more traditional food-related ministries: volunteering at food shelves, driving for Meals on Wheels, or establishing meal sites (any of which might make use of the church building); participating in CROP Hunger Walks; or supporting organizations such as Bread for the World, Heifer International, or any number of denominationally based domestic and global food justice organizations.

A faithful and effective leader will take on the prophetic role and lift up how God is present and active in these local efforts. Begin by identifying and celebrating what is already happening.

Some of these activities fly under the radar of the larger congregation. They take time, energy, and some level of passion to
accomplish—and they matter. Think of the person or people
who faithfully but quietly take care of the goods collected for
the food shelf each month, or the people who take time to wash
real dishes after fellowship so that less waste goes into the land-
fill, or those who are willing to take the extra time to trim the
landscaping and pick up leaves with human-powered tools rather
than noisy, fuming, gas-powered ones. Even in those simple,
seemingly mundane commitments, there exists positive, action-
able energy. Celebration, even of small steps forward, is a spark
that can motivate other actions. Remember Heffernan's words:
"You are never going to change the global food system. But you
can do this . . . and you have made a difference." And sometimes,
amazing things happen.

Two groups of local church people, one in the United States
and one in South Africa, made food and sustainability part of an
international bond of faith and friendship. The Shetek Conference of the Southwestern Minnesota Synod of the Evangelical
Lutheran Church in America (ELCA) developed a partnership with the Ondini Circuit of the Southeastern Diocese of
the Evangelical Lutheran Church of Southern Africa (ELCSA),
Zulu Christians living in KwaZulu-Natal. The partnership was
centered on fellowship and mutual understanding, but eventually, a significant aspect of this relationship grew around food
and sustainability. Leaders from the church in South Africa
sent a delegation to Minnesota to continue deepening their

relationship and to explore new ways to partner. The question was raised as to whether farmers from Minnesota might help assess and advise how land belonging to Zulu villages and churches might be put into food production. This part of South Africa was at the epicenter of the HIV/AIDS epidemic. Diabetes and HIV/AIDS were endemic in the Zulu villages. Diet and nutrition were poor, which contributed to the prevalence of diabetes and diminished the effectiveness of the medications to treat HIV/AIDS. The Zulu churches had significant holdings of land from grants by earlier governments—and after the end of apartheid, much land that had belonged to white South Africans was given back to the villages—but they did not have the experience or equipment to put it into production. Most of the church land had been rented out and was used for growing sugar cane, which did not benefit the nutritional needs of the community. A small group of Lutheran farmers from the Shetek Conference traveled to KwaZulu-Natal to discern with counterparts in the Ondini Circuit how the land might be stewarded and made productive for the sake of community health and nutrition. Today, large gardens have been established in some of the villages, with the hope of more to come. One garden in the village of Hoffenthal is particularly inspiring. It is cultivated by twelve *go-gos* (grandmas) who, working together with their American brothers and sisters, installed a simple irrigation system that has allowed them to grow fresh produce for their families. They sell the excess in the local market and use the profits to buy school uniforms, supplies, and other necessities for forty AIDS orphans.

Finding a Place at the Table

On every level—global, national, regional, and local—important decisions regarding food and sustainability are made that have huge impacts on people and communities. Major players, such as corporations, scientists, and large nongovernmental organizations (NGOs), are invited into the decision-making process by policy makers. They are granted a seat at the table to voice their opinions and influence outcomes. Unfortunately, faith-based organizations, including the church, often do not receive an invitation. Government policy makers often do not want to be bothered with faith-based ethics and think such contributions are not worthy of consideration—that only contributions based on science or economics are valid. Yet our biblical narrative and the communal ethics that grow out of it urgently need to be heard as decisions about food and sustainability are made. Thus people of faith must find a place at the table. That may mean finding gracious ways to invite ourselves.

On a national and international level, many Christian denominations and other faith traditions are issuing high-level statements on care of creation, climate change, and global hunger. This is one way the church's voice can be heard, though it is overly optimistic to believe that these perspectives find their way into the decision-making conversations. (It is difficult enough to get denominational members to read their own statements.) Nonetheless, it is important to proffer sound ethical arguments on these issues based on theological reflection. If the church doesn't do it, no one else will. At the least, church leaders can raise awareness that there is a biblical, theological, and ethical perspective to be considered in addition to a scientific and economic one. They can also inform people of faith who may actually find their way to those tables of decision-making. Pope Francis's encyclical *On Care for Our Common Home: Laudato si'* is one such document. By virtue of it coming from the pope, such a statement garners a lot of attention. The ELCA has three pertinent social statements: *Caring for Creation: Vision, Hope, and Justice* (1993), *Sufficient, Sustainable Livelihood for All* (1999), and *Genetics, Faith, and Responsibility* (2011). The website for the organization Interfaith Power and Light (https://www.interfaithpowerandlight.org) contains a resource page with links to statements by a variety of faith traditions.

As noted in chapter 3, these statements provide an opportunity for ecumenical understanding and action concerning food and environmental sustainability. They all have their detractors, but they are bold in their support for ongoing efforts to stem human abuse of the creation. The World Council of Churches (WCC), the Lutheran World Federation (LWF), and the ACT Alliance issued a joint declaration to the 2018 United Nations Climate Change Conference urging increased efforts to mitigate climate change and the impacts it has on global populations. LWF general secretary Rev. Dr. Martin Junge said, "As people of faith we know well how God wants this world to be and what God wants for human beings and calls them to be in this world. Our message to the churches and to the world is that creation is not for sale. As churches we should focus on that vision and engage in action for climate justice."[5]

Regional and local decision-making tables might be more accessible to those of us on the front lines of parish ministry.

These might include local boards, committees, or task forces that are making decisions about public green spaces or water supplies, zoning boundaries between agriculture and other uses, or land-use policies. It takes courage to invite yourself to these conversations when appropriate. It is equally important to use your voice in appropriate ways when at the table. You speak as a citizen of two realms: as a citizen of a secular government, representing yourself and perhaps others who share your point of view, and as a citizen of God's kingdom, witnessing to an ethic that values people and the nonhuman creation over political expediency or financial advantage. You can expect some people to be suspicious of your motivations as a "church person," wondering if you come with a religious (or even political) agenda. Keep in mind whom you represent and by what authority you speak. Christian leaders are perceived as speaking on behalf of the community of believers. Though this kind of public advocacy can be difficult, it can have a positive impact.

Let me share an example from my own experience. In one of the communities I served, large hog confinement facilities were prevalent and growing in number. Confinement operations are large buildings in which livestock are born and fed to attain market weight. In hog production, these buildings often hold between two thousand and four thousand animals each, which of course creates unique challenges for odor control and manure management and stresses the infrastructure of roads and water systems. The meat processing plants prefer to work with larger producers that are raising animals in controlled environments because, the processors claim, this ensures a reliable supply of consistently sized animals. Some plants process upward of twenty thousand animals a day and so require a large volume of hogs. The processors also prefer to precontract for animals, agreeing in advance to purchase animals from a particular producer, for a set price, provided they meet the strict requirements set by the processor. This contract arrangement is widespread in the poultry industry as well. This puts smaller-sized producers, many of whom fear being priced out of the market, at a distinct disadvantage. One might call the system the walmartization of pork production, or as economists call it, a monopsony—a monopoly that allows a single buyer to control a market.[6]

One congregation I served found itself in an uncomfortable situation created by this move to contract hog production and processing. Some of the farmers didn't think building massive confinement operations was the right thing to do. Many recognized the contracts were written heavily in favor of the processors. Other smaller farmers wanted to create a cooperative to increase production and compete for contracts with the larger producers. Many residents were angered by the prospect of more huge, smelly hog barns in the area. One of my parishioners was on the county planning and zoning board and was receiving angry phone calls from constituents. Folks representing all these categories of stakeholders, including some who worked in the processing plant, were present in the small congregation I served. They gathered around the altar for communion side by side. There was palpable tension, along with a lot of suspicion and inaccurate information, in the congregation and in the community. My immediate concern as a pastor was that these issues would divide the congregation.

Our local ministerium had been discussing the situation, because all our congregations were affected to some degree. We decided to invite ourselves to the table. Together, we represented nine congregations of four denominations in five small towns and the surrounding countryside. Our goals as an ecumenical organization were to provide a space for people from all sides to be heard, ensure that accurate information was being shared, and help maintain harmony in the community. We also were concerned that the producer/processor contracts unjustly favored the processor and that producers felt they had no choice but to enter into them or they would have no place to sell their hogs—the consequence of a local monopoly by the processor. This could be extremely detrimental to our local farmers and, by extension, to the community as a whole. We contacted some nonprofit organizations that were known to be astute about the environmental, public policy, and legal issues involved in these large-scale production arrangements. We offered to convene a public forum in the largest venue available in our community, the Catholic church.

Nearly three hundred people attended. Spokespeople from the nonprofits made presentations. A lawyer parsed an actual contract between a producer and the processing plant. Farmers with different perspectives spoke. A spokesperson from the processing plant gave a lengthy prepared statement and then left without taking questions. For those who remained, there were Q&A sessions and refreshments afterward. The gathering was civil and respectful. Perhaps the venue helped shape the tenor of the dialogue. In the end, some farmers decided against "going big" and signing contracts. Others opted to form a large cooperative with the processing plant.

A number of years later, one of my farmer parishioners who had opted into the cooperative came to me to talk. I had sensed at the time of the public forum that he was perturbed at what he perceived to be my meddling in things that were no business of a clergyperson. To his credit, he didn't allow that to interfere with his relationship with the church or with me. When he came to visit, he said, "Pastor, you were right about the contracts. Things were so stacked in favor of the plant. They controlled everything, and the coop failed." I assured him that it was never the goal to be right. Our concern as a ministerium was always that farmers be treated justly. At least some of our goals had been achieved: people were heard, good information was shared, and (generally) harmony was maintained in the larger community. And I believe that the church was seen as caring in a very practical way about those who grow our food. Yet ultimately, a number of hog farmers quit farming because they could no longer compete with the contract operations. This resulted in fewer and larger farms and fewer farmers, a loss that was felt by the entire community.

As discouraging as that story might be, we can conclude this chapter on a high note. In Milwaukee, in a poor, underserved, inner-city neighborhood is the Trickle Bee Café. It is a pay-what-you-can, not-for-profit café serving healthy meals made as much as possible with locally grown produce and rescued food—food from grocery stores that is safe to use but past the salable date. Everyone is welcomed. No one is turned away because they cannot pay. A ministry of the Moravian Church, it was born out of the vision of Rev. Christie Melby-Gibbons, who grew up in rural Iowa, and her husband, David, who is the head baker. They felt called to create a food ministry in the inner city. Their vision and motivation are inspiring:

> By providing fresh, healthy, locally-grown food to anyone regardless of ability to pay, we address food insecurity by feeding the immediate need of hunger, while providing resources to educate and inspire people to make a habit of healthy eating. Access to healthy food helps people to better care for themselves and their neighbors, which heals and strengthens community.
>
> We seek to be a peaceful gathering place in a neighborhood that has experienced much violence and neglect. We are a safe, inviting place for neighbors to gather to promote reconciliation and peace. We work to eliminate prejudice and discrimination against the economically and socially marginalized by creating a space where individuals from all backgrounds may gather around the concept of a community table.[7]

I had the privilege of visiting the Trickle Bee, meeting the Melby-Gibbonses, and volunteering in the kitchen. It is a remarkable place with a clientele that is both ethnically and economically diverse. Christie and David say that they are intentional about diversity, and it shows. They note that it took at least two years to establish trust in the neighborhood. Their neighbors' previous experience with "church people" involved mainly evangelists passing out tracts, not white Christians who wanted to live in and serve the neighborhood.

For Rev. Christie and David, their mission is not about converting people; it is about feeding people, body and spirit, and caring about food and community. This Christian caring is expressed in who they hire, who they serve, and what they serve. And so people gather around tables and share meals and stories. Rev. Christie and David and the employees and volunteers of the Trickle Bee Café are beautiful examples of incarnating hope and practicing the art of leadership for Christian ministry in a hungry world.

Questions for Reflection and Discussion

1. In what ways are you "tending the creation" in your backyard? How is your congregation or parish doing this? What have been the successes and frustrations?

2. How have you been carrying out the prophetic task given to all Christians to point out and celebrate what God is already doing in regard to food and sustainability?

3. If you and your congregation or parish could do more, what do you envision that being? What would you need to make that happen?

4. Do you believe the church should be represented at the tables of decision-making when it concerns food and sustainability? Why or why not?

5. What gives you hope, energy, and courage to be a Christian leader in a hungry world?

5

Cultivating Hope for
an Ongoing Harvest

In this concluding chapter, as we contemplate the future regarding food and sustainability, we must confront the most imminent and perplexing challenge ahead of us: global climate change. A corollary issue to climate change is the ongoing availability of water for drinking and agriculture.

Naming the Truth of Climate Change

The Intergovernmental Panel on Climate Change (IPCC), formed in 1988 by the United Nations, reviews current research and creates the most comprehensive reports on climate change worldwide. Their work undergirds the United Nations Framework Convention on Climate Change (UNFCCC), which oversees the Paris Agreement—the international effort to cap global warming. In 2019, the organization issued a report entitled *Climate Change and*

Land. Here are some of the key findings related to agriculture and food security:

- Observed climate change is already affecting food security through increasing temperatures, changing precipitation patterns, and greater frequency of some extreme events.
- Food security will be increasingly affected by projected future climate change.
- Vulnerability of pastoral systems (herding livestock) to climate change is very high.
- About 21–37% of total greenhouse gas (GHG) emissions are attributable to the food system.
- Agriculture and the food system are key to global climate change responses. Combining supply-side actions such as efficient production, transport, and processing with demand-side interventions such as modification of food choices, and reduction of food loss and waste, reduces GHG emissions and enhances food system resilience.[1]

These findings should be heard in the context of the most recent statistics on hunger and food insecurity from the Food and Agriculture Organization (FAO) of the United Nations:

Almost 690 million people in the world (8.9 percent of the world population) are estimated to have been undernourished in 2019. The number of people affected by hunger in the world continues to increase slowly. Latest estimates suggest that 9.7 percent of the world population (slightly less than 750 million people) was exposed to severe levels of food insecurity in 2019. An additional 16 percent of the world population, or more than 1.25 billion people, have experienced food insecurity at moderate levels. The prevalence of both moderate and severe levels of food insecurity (SDG [Sustainable Development Goal] Indicator 2.1.2) is estimated to be 25.9 percent in 2019 for the world as a whole. This translates into a total of 2 billion people.[2]

The FAO report notes that these food issues are "exacerbated by climate-related shocks." It is obvious that on a global level, climate change has been and will continue to be a major factor impacting agriculture and the production of food for a world that continues to suffer from hunger and food insecurity.

In the United States, the Global Change Research Act of 1990 requires the US Global Change Research Program (USGCRP) to deliver a report to Congress and the president no less than every four years. That report is called the *National Climate Assessment*, and the fourth edition was released in two volumes in 2017 and 2018. The second volume deals with the human welfare, societal, and environmental elements of climate change in the United States. Here are some key conclusions from that report related to food and sustainability. First, the authors address consequences for ecosystems in general: "Ecosystems and the benefits they provide to society are being altered by climate change, and these impacts are projected to continue. Many benefits provided by ecosystems and the environment, such as clean air and water, protection from coastal flooding, wood and fiber, crop pollination, hunting and fishing, tourism, cultural identities, and more will continue to be degraded by the impacts of climate change."[3]

These impacts will dramatically alter the lives and livelihoods of countless people in the United States. Later, focusing specifically on the effects of climate change on water, the authors state, "The quality and quantity of water available for use by people and eco-systems across the country are being affected by climate change, increasing risks and costs to agriculture, energy production, industry, recreation, and the environment."[4] These observations and predictions are alarming. One can feel a sense of urgency as the scientists speak of necessities fundamental to life and well-being becoming "jeopardized by the impacts of climate change."

The report also speaks directly to the effects of climate change on American agriculture: "Rising temperatures, extreme heat, drought, wildfire on rangelands, and heavy downpours are expected to increasingly disrupt agricultural productivity in the United States. Expected increases in challenges to livestock health, declines in crop yields and quality, and changes in extreme events in the United States and abroad threaten rural livelihoods, sustainable food security, and price stability. . . . Overall, yields from major U.S. crops are expected to decline as a consequence of increases in temperatures and possibly changes in water availability, soil erosion, and disease and pest outbreaks."[5] Increasing temperatures, changing precipitation patterns, and expanding soil erosion will significantly reduce the land's capacity to grow crops and support livestock grazing. Though both the FAO and the USGCRP make recommendations about how to mitigate the predicted outcomes, they also emphasize that not enough is happening now. Hence the outlook is grim.

In particular, the availability and safety of water for personal consumption and agricultural use has not been a high-priority concern aside from the water-quality disaster that began in 2014 in Flint, Michigan, which was largely a result of neglected infrastructure and political inaction. For many experts attuned to water issues, a major worry is the private, corporate acquisition of water rights for profit. During a meeting of the Rural Church Network of the United States and Canada, held in Washington, DC, in the early 2000s, participants met with leaders of a nongovernmental organization (NGO) called Food and Water Watch. They are one of a number of NGOs monitoring the private acquisition and control of water sources nationally and globally. The mission statement of Food and Water Watch begins, "Our food, water and climate are under constant assault by corporations who put profit over the survival of humanity."[6] In that meeting, we learned that many multinational corporations are buying up water rights, especially in the Global North and South, in anticipation of shortages triggered by climate change. The sale of these rights, often by corrupt government officials without the local population's knowledge, will disadvantage those communities that now have to pay for resources to which they previously had public access.

At the time of our meeting, the activity of these corporations had gone on largely unnoticed and unchallenged by the public. Some in the scientific community have given this more attention recently and have even taken to characterizing these corporate acquisitions as "water grabbing."[7] A 2013 *Scientific American* article asserts, "The 'water grabbing' by corporations amounts to 454 billion cubic meters per year globally, according to a new study by environmental scientists. That's about 5 percent of the water the world uses annually."[8]

In the United States, many local communities are privatizing their public water systems, selling them to for-profit companies, which often increases the cost of water to the citizenry 60 percent or more, a burdensome expense for low-income residents. Some larger, growing urban areas are also buying up water rights in surrounding rural—primarily agricultural—areas to meet the water demands of the increasing urban population. In environments where agriculture is dependent on irrigation, this is exceedingly problematic.

In 2019, I witnessed the privatization issue firsthand while attending the annual meeting of the Rural Chaplains Association in Crowley County, Colorado, the poorest county in Colorado. County residents were selling their water rights, surface water and aquifer water, to the growing "front range" cities of the Rocky Mountains, like Pueblo, Colorado. They sold because they needed the money. But a local reporter quoted one former farmer: "When we sold our water, we sold our future."[9] We heard directly from some ranchers that they had to compete with these urban areas for water for their crops and livestock during an ongoing drought that was the result of high temperatures and below-average rainfall. The reasons the availability and control of water are vital for food and sustainability should be obvious. Just as everyone must eat (and have water to grow the food they consume), everyone must drink.

The effects of climate change on access to water, growing food, and sustaining the creation are bleak on their own. Adding to these grim forecasts is the complicating factor of those who downplay or outright deny the reality of climate change. Even some highly placed appointed and elected officials of the very government that commissioned the *National Climate Assessment* refute this information. This has become such an obstacle to productive responses to climate change that academic studies have examined the phenomenon,[10] and NASA has needed to issue statements such as this: "Multiple studies published in peer-reviewed scientific journals show that 97 percent or more of actively publishing climate scientists agree: Climate-warming trends over the past century are extremely likely due to human activities. In addition, most of the leading scientific organizations worldwide have issued public statements endorsing this position."[11]

People who downplay and deny climate change are members of our congregations and communities. Like much of our contemporary public discourse, discussion and debate around climate change can become divisive and polarized. Climate change denial exacerbates that polarization. When facing the issues affecting food and sustainability in the context of ministry, we need to be ready to faithfully and productively engage with those who have not yet accepted the fact of global warming and climate change. The challenge is to engage, holding true to the facts, but in ways that do not contribute to further division and polarization. So this is what we face: climate change driven by global warming, which scientists call "among the greatest threats of our generation—and of generations to come—to public health, ecosystems, and the economy."[12] The IPCC concludes, "Global temperatures could reach an irreversible tipping point in just 12 years if the world doesn't act dramatically to reduce the amount of carbon dioxide released into the atmosphere."[13]

Even though some would deny the truth, we are seeing some of the physical manifestations of the impending tipping point now in the form of unprecedented weather events and natural disasters. Australia experienced historic wildfires in the 2019–20 fire season, burning 72,000 square miles and killing or displacing nearly three billion animals. In 2020, amid historic heatwaves, California experienced its worst wildfire season ever in terms of acres destroyed—over 4.2 million acres of federal and state land combined. The 2021 wildfire season is currently outpacing the record year of 2020. Central Iowa in the summer of 2020 experienced a historic derecho with category 1 to category 4 hurricane-force winds for nearly an hour, devastating communities and destroying ten million acres of crops. According to the National Oceanic and Atmospheric Administration (NOAA), the 2020 Atlantic hurricane season "produced 30 named storms [the most on record] . . . of which 14 became hurricanes [the second-highest number on record]."[14] NOAA predicts that the 2021 season will be significantly more active than normal. Nearly 40 percent of the country is experiencing moderate to severe drought affecting an estimated seventy-seven million people. So from the perspective of ministry, when such realities can easily paralyze us in fear, what do we do? How do we engage these realities in faithful and effective ways as God's people? We turn to hope.

Cultivating Hope

In the introduction, I said that the process of writing this book has drawn me into an arduous journey to find hope. In the fourth chapter, I made the argument that hope is a key ingredient of the art of leadership for Christian ministry in a hungry world—the energy that empowers people to persevere as well as take on God's challenge to do justice, love kindness, and walk humbly with their God. In light of the issues impacting food and sustainability described in the first chapter and the imminent future of global climate change described in this chapter, how do we cultivate hope? Here is what I found.

Wendell Berry has long worked for change in the extraordinarily complex food system that has developed in the United States and globally and the attendant environmental crises that have emerged. He has done so as a writer, speaker, teacher, and farmer. More than forty years ago, he wrote in a seminal book, *The Unsettling of America: Culture and Agriculture,* "The care of the Earth is our most ancient and most worthy, and after all our most pleasing responsibility. To cherish what remains of it and to foster its renewal is *our only legitimate hope.*"[15] After thirty-five years of thoughtful yet practical activism, Berry was interviewed for the radio show *YaleEnvironment360.* After reflecting on the work he had been engaged in over the years, the subject turned to hope:

E360: I've heard you describing the difference between optimism and hope, and you said that in terms of the issues you really care about, you would not describe yourself as optimistic but as hopeful. Can you explain that?

Berry: The issue of hope is complex, and the sources of hope are complex. The things hoped for tend to be specific and, to imply an agenda of work, things that can be done. Optimism is a general program that things are going to come out swell, pretty much whether we help out or not. This is largely unjustified by circumstances and history.[16]

I find Berry's words about hope, rooted in years of experience, inspiring and instructive. Hope is much more than the state of mind of optimism. Hope begets action, specific work, things that can be done—caring responsibility that fosters the renewal of God's earth.

I encountered a similar perspective on hope in author David W. Orr, professor of environmental studies and politics at Oberlin College. He was the motivating force behind the design, funding, and construction of the college's Adam Joseph Lewis Center, which was named by an American Institute of Architects panel in 2010 as "the most important green building of the past 30 years" and as "one of 30 milestone buildings of the twentieth century" by the US Department of Energy. In the aptly named *Hope Is an Imperative: The Essential David Orr,* author David W. Orr offers a practical perspective on hope: "*Hope* is a verb with its sleeves rolled up. In contrast to optimism or despair, hope requires that one actually do something to improve the world. Authentic hope comes with an imperative to act. There is no such thing as passive hope."[17] At the end of the book, he asserts,

> Hope, however, requires us to check our optimism at the door and enter the future without illusions. It requires a level of honesty, self-awareness, and sobriety that is difficult to summon and sustain. I know a great many smart people and many very good people, but I know far fewer people who can handle hard truth gracefully without despairing. . . . Authentic hope, in other words, is made of sterner stuff than optimism. It must be rooted in the truth as best we can see it, knowing that our vision is always partial. Hope requires the courage to reach farther, dig deeper, confront our limits and those of nature, work harder, and dream dreams. . . . Hope, authentic hope, can be found only in our capacity to discern the truth about our situation and ourselves and summon the fortitude to act accordingly. *We have it on high authority that the Truth will set us free* from illusion, greed, and ill will and per-haps, with a bit of luck, from self-imposed destruction.[18]

I find it remarkable—and delightful—that in this scholarly treat-ment of environmental issues, Orr gives us a clear allusion to John 8:31–32. In doing so, he implies that authentic hope is rooted in a truth more profound than scientific facts.

I believe that Orr and Berry are describing the hope we need to confront the challenges facing food and sustainability, a hope that is rooted in the Truth. We need a hope that rises above mere optimism, a hope that gives us the courage to reach farther and dream for a just and sustainable future for the creation and all who must eat. We need a hope that demands and empowers action, a hope that rolls up its sleeves and gets to work. We need a hope that, in the apostle Paul's words of encouragement, is born out of suffering, endurance, and character—a hope that does not disappoint (Rom 5:3–5). We as the church, the body of Christ, can cultivate that hope.

Cultivating Hope by Reshaping Narratives

One important way the church can cultivate hope is to propagate a unifying narrative that allows people from different places and perspectives to understand one another and work together toward shared purposes. In chapter 2, based on the work of Tex Sample, I lifted up the significant role that narrative and stories play, especially in a small-town and rural culture. By *narrative*, I mean "a way of presenting or understanding a situation or series of events that reflects and promotes a particular point of view or set of values."[19] Individual stories contribute to, build, and shape the overarching narrative. I like to think of narrative as the song we sing together, and stories are the verses that make up the song.

For realistic positive change to happen related to food and sustainability issues, those who grow our food and those who eat that food need to work together for a common purpose. The resulting shared narrative can revolve around the simple reality that everyone must eat, a narrative in which God is deeply invested, as highlighted in chapter 3.

Many narratives and stories related to the issues of food and sustainability tend to polarize. For example,

- People in the cities don't care about what's happening in rural places.
- Livestock farming is cruel to animals.
- Farming hurts the environment.
- That political party wants to take away your hamburger or your land.
- City people don't know what it takes to grow the food on their table.
- Rural people are backward.
- There's nothing out there in the countryside.
- Why would anyone want to live in a crowded city?
- Climate change is a hoax.
- Global warming isn't that big of a deal.
- Someone who doesn't believe in global warming is ignorant.

Such beliefs represent untrue or only partially true narratives that are unhelpful and push us into opposing groups. The narratives they represent need to be refuted or reshaped in ways that empower people to work together for common goals.

Let me offer an example. I was once invited to participate in a series of Sunday morning adult forums sponsored by a large suburban congregation in Minneapolis. The topic was food and care of creation. The presenters included a state senator, a representative of the food company General Mills, a professor of plant genetics from the University of Minnesota, and me. I noticed that no farmer was present, and so I took it upon myself to represent the rural perspective. Each Sunday, one of the presenters would speak, and then there would be a panel discussion by the presenters, followed by a question-and-answer session with congregational participants.

One Sunday, in the question-and-answer time, a parishioner asserted (I'm paraphrasing), "Farmers are tearing out windbreaks and using more chemicals and bigger machines, and they are ruining the environment. All they care about is making more money." You could feel the tension in the room. I received that as a partially true statement that was not helpful for building the shared narrative that this event was seeking—namely, that those who grow food and those who eat food need to find ways to support one another while caring for God's creation. So I responded by acknowledging that many agricultural practices are hard on the environment, but many farmers are working with government agencies and soil and water conservationists to improve those practices. I also added that it was not true that farmers do not care about God's creation. To make that fact more palatable, I told the story of Fox Hill.

As a pastor, I made it a practice to ride along in tractors with some of my farmer parishioners during spring planting and fall harvest. One spring, I noticed a huge pile of stones in the middle of the field we were planting. It was obvious that the farmer had plowed around the pile and was now planting around it and would have to harvest around it in the fall. Normally, farmers pick the rocks out of their fields and place them in a corner so they are out of the way. This pile was a big inconvenience and was taking up usable crop ground, so I asked why it was there. The farmer said (I paraphrase),

Oh, we call that Fox Hill. Almost every year, there is a den of fox pups in those rocks. It has been there as long as I can remember. My grandfather used to take me out here every spring when I was old enough to ride in the tractor, and we would watch for the baby foxes playing. That has been a tradition for my kids and now my grandkids. I've thought of moving those damn rocks, but I'd miss the foxes. They need a place to live and raise their family too. So I just keep throwing more rocks on it.

I concluded this story for the Sunday series by observing that most farmers care about raising good food and taking care of the land so they can pass something good on to the next generation. Fox Hill was just one example of that.

Almost immediately, the mood in the room and the tenor of the conversation changed, softened. After the forum, three or four people came up to me and told me that they either had grown up on a farm or had grandparents who farmed. My story confirmed what they had remembered: The farmers cared about the land. It was not just about the money. One said she thought an important conversation had begun in those forums. She thought their congregation needed to talk about what they could do together to improve the system of food for everyone, including the creation. And she said, "Those of us who have rural roots need to tell our story."

We as church know how to tell stories. We know their power. Our faith tradition ties us to a narrative that is many millennia old. We can use that knowledge to create opportunities to build a shared narrative that declares everyone must eat, and therefore, we need sustainable systems to make that happen. We need to listen to one another's stories, refute what is false, and affirm what is true. We need to lift up and retell those stories that give us a collective hope with its sleeves rolled up so that together we can enact change for justice and sustainability for God's creation.

Cultivating Hope by Building Relationships

A second means by which the church can cultivate hope that empowers action is to build relationships that personally connect those who grow food with those who do not. In actuality, relationships will begin to develop organically as a shared narrative emerges. But just as food in the garden needs to be tended to bear fruit, so it is with cross-context relationships, which are often challenged by distance and time demands. Again, as I presented in chapter 2, based on the research of Tex Sample, interpersonal relationships affect how moral issues are engaged and how action for change is carried out. This is especially true for people in small-town and rural communities. Sample says, "An issue that comes up will be considered in terms of the family and communal ties one has. A moral issue will be considered in the light of these same kinship and local connections. Any attempt at social change will need to be grounded in such relationships, and religious beliefs will be understood much more in relational than discursive ways."[20]

Apart from relationships, some issues can seem distant and abstract and therefore more open to divisive and polarizing discourse. In the context of relationships, issues become personal, and most people tend to become more thoughtful and considerate. Also, effective social change is usually achieved through collective action. Individuals can make a difference. But long-lasting systemic change involving the concerns of food, sustainability, and climate change will require the joint efforts of many people. Such change involves networks of relationships.

Let me share another example. When I would speak at education events or guest preach in metropolitan congregations, I would often talk about care of creation and the difficult circumstances of those who grow our food. Afterward, listeners would ask, "What can we do to help?" I encouraged them to get to know some people who farm. One way to do that is to buy vegetables and fruit, meat, and eggs directly from them because more of your food dollar goes to the farmer. In many metropolitan areas, community- or congregational-supported agriculture (CSA) networks or farmers' markets encourage such relationships.

In spite of my own good advice, I was confronted with the challenge of building relationships for the farmers in my context—one without nearby metropolitan areas that would provide a direct market. My farmers primarily raised hogs and beef. In talking to people I would meet in St. Paul and Minneapolis churches, I came to believe they would love to buy beef directly from my farmers, especially if the cattle were "raised healthy"— without artificial hormones or antibiotics and on pasture, not in stockyards. In fact, they would pay a premium for that kind of meat. I then had to convince some of my farmers to take a risk and change the way they raised their animals. As we did the calculations, we determined the folks in the Twin Cities would get chemical-free meat for less than they would pay for a similar product in the store. The farmers would make a consistent profit on each animal they raised, which was not guaranteed if they sold them on the open market.

It seemed like a win-win to me. But it did not get going until we could build relationships between my farmers and the people who would buy from them. So we took some of our farmers to visit sister congregations in the Twin Cities, and we brought people from the cities to visit the farmer's congregations and the farms themselves. Thus was born Holy Cows, so named because it was a beef-marketing network developed through congregations. It did not have a huge impact, but it made a difference. The network has helped sustain some of those farmers as well as the families of two local butchers who cut and package the meat. It has resulted in some animals being raised in healthier and more creation-friendly ways. But the most enduring blessing is not the economics but the holy relationships that have been established and continue—that have changed a tiny piece of the food system for the better.

In order to accomplish a more just food system and maintain a healthier planet, we will need each other—and the church knows how to do relationship as well. In fact, the church is built on relationship. As Jesus compels us, "Just as I have loved you, you also should love one another" (John 13:34). Any good relationship takes time and commitment, of course. But when people better understand and are committed to one another, they are more willing to work together. In that is great hope.

Cultivating Hope by Acting with Younger Generations

Finally, I propose a rather bold way for the church to cultivate hope. I believe the church needs to engage the energy and activism of younger generations on the issues of food, sustainability, and climate change. This is an extension of my call to cultivate hope by reshaping narratives and building relationships, but to do so with the generations that follow us. Significant research into the characteristics of the millennial and Gen Z generations shows that a high percentage of them are not connected to the church, and many do not feel the church is relevant. We, as the church, have been waiting for these generations to come back to us. Current research seems to indicate that this will not happen.[21] Research also indicates that these generations care deeply about the issues that are the focus of this book.[22] So I believe that we should stop waiting for these generations to come to us and should instead turn to them.

The concerns with which we have been grappling in this book are first-order issues to these generations—matters that directly affect their hopes for the future. We need to listen to them. At the age of sixteen, Greta Thunberg, a Swedish student, started a school boycott in order to focus on what she believes to be the most important issue facing her generation: climate change. In December 2018, she spoke to the United Nations Climate Change Summit. Her words are a powerful call to action:

> I shouldn't be up here. I should be back in school on the other side of the ocean. Yet you all come to us young people for hope. How dare you! You have stolen my dreams

and my childhood with your empty words. . . . For more than 30 years, the science has been crystal clear. How dare you continue to look away and come here saying that you're doing enough, when the politics and solutions needed are still nowhere in sight. You say you hear us and that you understand the urgency. But no matter how sad and angry I am, I do not want to believe that. Because if you really understood the situation and still kept on failing to act, then you would be evil. And that I refuse to believe. You are failing us. But the young people are starting to understand your betrayal. The eyes of all future generations are upon you. And if you choose to fail us, I say: We will never forgive you. We will not let you get away with this. Right here, right now is where we draw the line. The world is waking up. And change is coming, whether you like it or not.[23]

Together, we as the church, young and old, need to go to where younger generations gather, go to where they protest, go to where they march. We need to listen to and be willing to equip and encourage them to lead on these issues. Then we need to follow their lead. The whole church needs to join them in action. What we need is a movement in the church similar to what happened in the civil rights movement of the 1950s and 1960s. Black churches in particular joined that movement. They hosted meetings, joined marches and rallies, and gave emotional, physical, and spiritual support to those on the front lines. And change happened. There is much energy and passionate concern over the pending disaster of climate change among younger generations. The UN has noted this as a global trend: "The need to include youth voices has become more pressing than ever as young people, whose futures are threatened by accelerating global heating, are increasingly demanding action towards a more just, equitable, and climate-resilient society."[24] Perhaps, if we add the church's energy to theirs, we can begin to affect meaningful change. And perhaps the church will begin to feel relevant to them.

For my part, I am listening to and learning from the young adults in my orbit. Not all of them are connected to the church. I'm listening to and learning from my niece, Taylor, who is educating herself in the science and sociology of sustainable food systems and who steered me to the website Civil Eats (https://civileats.com), "a daily source for critical thought about the American food system." I'm listening to and learning from my theological students, many of whom are integrating their biblical-theological studies with these sustainability issues. I'm listening to and learning from my adult children and their spouses and significant others as they modify their lifestyles to reflect their concern for the creation in many small but important ways—buying "ugly food" that has been rejected by the commercial market and would otherwise go to waste, using compostable tableware, growing their own food and sharing it, and making many other intentional changes. In all of them, I see tangible signs of the verb *hope* with its sleeves rolled up, and I am inspired to join them.

Conclusion

As I write the last words of this book, we are living in the ongoing, anxiety-ridden uncertainty of the Covid-19 global pandemic. Much of this book has been written during the time of Covid-19. I have chosen not to draw that reality into the earlier chapters of this work because it would further complicate—in ways we do not yet fully understand—the already complicated issues I am addressing. I will say this, though: it is humbling to contemplate that a tiny element of God's creation, a virus invisible to the naked eye, has the power to disrupt the entire globe. That virus has also exposed some of the key vulnerabilities of the complex globalized food system with which we live. The people who pick our food, the people who process our food, the people who sell us our food, and the people who prepare and serve our food in restaurants are all essential to our society and are at substantially higher risk of contracting Covid-19 as they make sure we can eat. People in the Global North and South, where food systems are very fragile, are suffering more because of the virus. And as food establishments and food services are shut down and demand for food diminishes, farmers are suffering another blow in a long siege of economic trauma. But this virus has given us a glimmer of hope as well. As economies have intentionally slowed down, we have seen the immediate positive environmental impact. If we pay attention, this shows us that we can change our behaviors in ways that will improve the health of God's creation. We can do what needs to be done.

Today is the World Day of Prayer for the Care of Creation. It marks the beginning of the ecumenical Season of Creation: Jubilee for the Earth, which recognizes the fiftieth anniversary of Earth Day. Today Pope Francis, author of *Laudato si': On Care for Our Common Home*, said this: "[The pandemic] . . . has given us the chance to develop new ways of living. . . . The pandemic has brought us to a crossroads. We must use this decisive moment to end our superfluous and destructive goals and activities and to cultivate values, connections and activities that are lifegiving. We must examine our habits of energy usage, consumption, transportation, and diet. We must eliminate the superfluous and destructive aspects of our economies and nurture life-giving ways to trade, produce and transport goods."[25]

As the leader of the world's 1.2 billion Roman Catholics, Pope Francis has been a bold and influential voice speaking out for societal change to improve the environmental health of the earth. It is insightful that he points to this time of pandemic as an opportunity to make changes for the sake of the well-being of God's creation.

Finally, on this day, my second grandchild, Simon John, was born. I am in the final trimester of my life. He and his sister—my first grandchild, Magdalena—are just beginning theirs. Will we as a society make the changes necessary so that they and all those of their generation may live in a healthy, just creation— one where everyone must eat? Will we, as the church, lead that change? I pray that this book might contribute in some small way toward that end.

Questions for Reflection and Discussion

1. In the face of the difficult realities named in this chapter and elsewhere in the book, what gives you hope? Why?

2. In your community or congregation, what narratives related to food, sustainability, or climate change need reshaping? How might you do that?

3. What are some tangible ways that you could build relationships that cultivate hopeful action related to the issues discussed in this book?

4. What are some tangible ways you can join with and encourage younger generations in hopeful action for the sake of the health of the creation? How can you invite your congregation to join with you in that endeavor?

5. What are two or three key takeaways for you from *Everyone Must Eat*?

ACKNOWLEDGMENTS

This work is one more step in a long journey being undertaken by many faithful and dedicated thinkers and doers who, over the past half century or so, have confronted the reality that human beings have impacted our planet in devastating ways and that an ever-growing global population needs to eat. They have also proclaimed that God cares about such things. I have joined their journey and added my voice to theirs. I am deeply appreciative of what they have taught me and how they have inspired me.

There are two fellow sojourners that I would like to thank here: C. Dean Freudenberger and Alvin Luedke. Dean took me under his wing and invited me into this network of thinkers and doers and shared with me his wisdom based on decades of work in global agricultural, environmental, theological mission and reflection. Alvin guided me through my thesis work. He and I have been teaching colleagues in the discipline of theological education for small-town and rural ministry, which we like to say makes us out standing in a very narrow field. I thank God for the ways in which these two have been and continue to be blessings to me and the mission of God's church.

When I first began serving as a pastor in a rural context, I knew virtually nothing about farming. My parishioners graciously and patiently taught me about the land. They turned me into an advocate for those who tend the land and grow our food. They gave me the privilege of being their pastor. I felt challenged by the issues facing the communities I served. I fell in love with the people and the land, and I stayed. This book could never have been imagined if not for their love, encouragement, and critique. I hope it honors their important role in our society. In addition, I would like to thank Beth Gaede, my editor, for her patience and wise guidance in bringing this book to fruition.

Throughout the writing of this book, my family kept me grounded in what the issues of food justice and sustainability mean for real people. They loved me through the process—gave me space when needed, pressed me at other times, read and offered feedback. My adult children have social justice in their veins. They have traveled to many places in the world, with their parents and on their own, not as tourists but as world citizens. Together we have seen the issues of this book lived out globally in very real ways. All of that is anchored by my life partner, soulmate, and fellow world traveler, Margaret. She has taught me the beauty and practicality of agape. And she has helped me see these issues through feminist eyes.

Finally, I trust, "the earth is the Lord's and all that is in it, the world, and those who live in it" (Ps 24:1).

NOTES

INTRODUCTION

1 Christopher J. H. Wright, *God's People in God's Land: Family, Land, and Property in the Old Testament* (Grand Rapids: William B. Eerdmans, 1990), 3.

CHAPTER 1

1 Tim Marema, "Census Bureau Shines Spotlight on Rural America, Gives Close Look at Changes in Demography, Work," *Northern Kentucky Tribune*, December 20, 2016, https://tinyurl.com/p7u6r4y7.

2 *Encyclopedia Britannica Online*, s.v. "rural society," last modified October 23, 2017, https://www.britannica.com/topic/rural-society.

3 John Baldwin, "Rural Culture," *Cultural Comparisons COM 272* (blog), June 28, 2012, https://culturalcomparisonscom272.wordpress.com/urban-rural/rural-culture.

4 *Merriam-Webster*, s.v. "ecosystem," accessed June 29, 2018, https://www.merriam-webster.com/dictionary/ecosystem.

5 William Heffernan, *Report to the National Farmers Union: Consolidation in the Food and Agriculture System* (Washington, DC: National Farmers Union, 1999).

6 Paul Harris, "Monsanto Sued Small Farmers to Protect Seed Patents, Report Says," *Guardian*, February 12, 2013, https://www.theguardian.com/environment/2013/feb/12/monsanto-sues-farmers-seed-patents.

7 Wolfram Schlenker and Sofia B. Villas-Boas, "Consumer and Market Responses to Mad Cow Disease," *American Journal of Agricultural Economics* 91, no. 4 (November 2009): 1140–41.

8 Philip H. Howard, *Concentration and Power in the Food System: Who Controls What We Eat?* (London: Bloomsbury Academic, 2016), 71–163.

9 Howard, 154.

10 "These People Own the Most Land in America," 24/7 Wall St., MSN, January 26, 2021, https://tinyurl.com/w578r7tj.

11 Peter Jackson, *Anxious Appetites: Food and Consumer Culture* (London: Bloomsbury Academic, 2015), 193–94.

12 Wright, *God's People in God's Land*, 3 (emphasis added).

13 Scott Baldauf, "Texas Ranchers Sue Oprah for Bad-Mouthing Burgers," *Christian Science Monitor*, January 8, 1998, https://www.csmonitor.com/1998/0108/010898.us.us.5.html.

14 "New USDA Report Breaks Down U.S. Food Recalls 2004–2013," *FoodSafety Magazine*, April 25, 2018, https://www.food-safety.com/articles/5764-new-usda-report-breaks-down-us-food-recalls-2004-2013.

15 Paula Dutko, Michele Ver Ploeg, and Tracey Farrigan, *Characteristics and Influential Factors of Food Deserts*, Economic Research Report no. 140, USDA, August 2012, https://www.ers.usda.gov/webdocs/publications/45014/30940_err140.pdf, 5.

16 Michele Ver Ploeg, David Nulph, and Ryan Williams, "Mapping Food Deserts in the United States," *Amber Waves: The Economics of Food, Farming, Natural Resources, and Rural America*, USDA Economic Research Service, December 1, 2011, https://www.ers.usda.gov/amber-waves/2011/december/data-feature-mapping-food-deserts-in-the-us/.

17 "New CDC Report: More Than 100 Million Americans Have Diabetes or Prediabetes," Centers for Disease Control and Prevention,

July 18, 2017, https://www.cdc.gov/media/releases/2017/p0718 -diabetes-report.html.

18 Robert Kenner, dir., *Food, Inc.* (New York: Magnolia Pictures, 2008).

19 Eric Holt-Giménez, "We Already Grow Enough Food for 10 Billion People—and Still Can't End Hunger," HuffPost, December 18, 2014, https://www.huffpost.com/entry/world-hunger_n_1463429.

20 Sara M. Allinder and Janet Fleischman, "The World's Largest HIV Epidemic in Crisis: HIV in South Africa," Center for Strategic and International Studies, accessed November 11, 2019, https://tinyurl .com/3e5b9sjx.

21 "Gulf of Mexico 'Dead Zone' Is the Largest Ever Measured," National Oceanic and Atmospheric Association, US Department of Commerce, August 2, 2017, https://www.noaa.gov/media-release/ gulf-of-mexico-dead-zone-is-largest-ever-measured.

22 Martin D. Smith et al., "Seafood Prices Reveal Impacts of a Major Ecological Disturbance," *PNAS* 114, no. 7 (2017): 1512–17, https:// www.pnas.org/content/114/7/1512.

23 Rachel Carson, *Silent Spring*, 50th anniversary ed. (Boston: Houghton Mifflin, 2002), 189 (emphasis added).

24 Wendell Berry, *The Unsettling of America: Culture and Agriculture*, 1st Counterpoint ed. (Berkeley, CA: Counterpoint, 2015), 178.

25 David Shukman, "China Cloning on an 'Industrial Scale,'" BBC News, January 14, 2014, https://www.bbc.com/news/science -environment-25576718.

26 Adrianna Diaz, "To Fill Organ Donation Gap in China, Doctors Turn to Surprising Source," CBS News, February 18, 2017, https:// tinyurl.com/zxhrx5bc.

27 "Smithfield's Plan for Pig-to-Human Transplant Parts," CBS News, April 12, 2017, https://www.cbsnews.com/news/smithfield-plan-for -pig-to-human-transplant-parts.

28 Harris, "Monsanto Sued Small Farmers."

29 Bill Freese and Martha Crouch, *Monarchs in Peril: Herbicide-Resistant Crops and the Decline of Monarch Butterflies in North America* (Washington, DC: Center for Food Safety, 2015).

30 Tamar Haspal, "Illegal Immigrants Help Fuel U.S. Farms. Does Affordable Produce Depend on Them?," *Washington Post*, March 17, 2017, https://tinyurl.com/7s6k5ken.

31 Padma Lakshmi, "Undocumented Immigrants Make Your Food," interview by Samantha Bee, *Full Frontal with Samantha Bee*, August 15, 2018.

32 Heffernan, *Consolidation*, 1, 16.

CHAPTER 2

1 Suzanne Smith, "The Institutional and Intellectual Origins of Rural Sociology" (paper presented to the 74th Annual Meeting of the Rural Sociological Society, Boise, ID, 2011), 5.

2 *Merriam-Webster*, s.v. "agriculture," accessed February 28, 2018, https://www.merriam-webster.com/dictionary/agriculture.

3 *Merriam-Webster*, s.v. "culture," accessed February 28, 2018, https://www.merriam-webster.com/dictionary/culture.

4 Mark Pagel, "Does Language Bring Us Together or Pull Us Apart?," *TED Radio Hour*, December 13, 2013.

5 Wendell Berry, "The Culture of Agriculture" (lecture, Agriculture for a Small Planet Symposium, Spokane, WA, July 1, 1974).

6 Berry.

7 Martin Luther King Jr., *The Strength to Love: Gift Edition* (Minneapolis: Fortress Press, 2013), 13.

8 Lawrence W. Farris, *The Dynamics of Small Town Ministry* (Lanham, MD: Rowman & Littlefield, 2014), 17–24.

9 A one-hundred-year flood does not mean an intensity of flooding that only happens every one hundred years. It means there is a one in one hundred (or 1 percent) chance of this magnitude of flooding happening in any given year. Thus a five-hundred-year flood has a .2 percent chance of happening in any given year.

10 Kent R. Hunter, *The Lord's Harvest and the Rural Church: A New Look at Ministry in the Agri-culture* (Kansas City: Beacon Hill Press, 1993).

11 Debbie Weingarten, "Why Are America's Farmers Killing Themselves?," *Guardian*, December 11, 2018, https://tinyurl.com/3359kp8v.

12 Herbert Muschamp, "Eloquent Champion of the Vernacular Landscape," Architecture View, *New York Times*, April 21, 1996.

13 Tex Sample, *Ministry in an Oral Culture: Living with Will Rogers, Uncle Remus, and Minnie Pearl* (Louisville: Westminster John Knox, 1994), 6.

14 Sample, 4.

15 Sample, 3.

16 Sample, 5, 30.

17 Juergen Voegele, "For up to 800 Million Rural Poor, a Strong World Bank Commitment to Agriculture," World Bank, November 12, 2014, https://tinyurl.com/3th3hwvu.

18 I have found my observations about rural/urban differences regarding space and place and my subsequent observations concerning differences regarding rural/urban approaches to time affirmed in the writings of Wendell Berry, Carol Bly, Kent Hunter, Kathleen Norris, Tex Sample, and others. Some of the best sociological research on this has been done in Europe—for example, Marcel Hunziker, Matthias Buchecker, and Terry Hartig, "Space and Place—Two Aspects of the Human-Landscape Relationship," in *A Changing World: Challenges for Landscape Research*, ed. F. Kienast, O. Wildi, and S. Ghosh (Dordrecht, Netherlands: Springer, 2007), 47–62; and Michael Woods, "Conceptualizing Rural Areas in Metropolitan Society: A Rural View" (paper, Aberystwyth University, Aberystwyth, Wales, n.d.), https://sites.nationalacademies.org/cs/groups/dbassesite/documents/webpage/dbasse_167038.pdf.

19 Wright, *God's People in God's Land*, 3.

CHAPTER 3

1 Walter Brueggemann, *Genesis, Interpretation: A Bible Commentary for Teaching and Preaching* (Atlanta: John Knox, 1982), 16–17.

2 Linda Gradstein, "Saving the Planet through Religious Cooperation," Media Line, Ynet News, November 11, 2014, https://www.ynetnews.com/articles/0,7340,L-4590203,00.html. Please note, the gender-specific language is theirs, not mine.

3 Walter Brueggemann, *Genesis: Interpretation* (Louisville: Westminster John Knox, 1986), 32.

4 James Limburg, "The Responsibility of Royalty: Genesis 1–11 and the Care of the Earth," *Word and World* 11, no. 2 (Spring 1991): 126.

5 Limburg, 127.

6 *Merriam-Webster*, s.v. "trust," accessed May 15, 2018, https://www.merriam-webster.com/dictionary/trust.

7 *Merriam-Webster*, s.v. "covenant," accessed May 15, 2018, https://www.merriam-webster.com/dictionary/covenant.

8 Patrick Miller, *Deuteronomy, Interpretation: A Bible Commentary for Teaching and Preaching* (Atlanta: John Knox, 1982), 50.

9 Miller, 52.

10 Ellen F. Davis, *Scripture, Culture, and Agriculture: An Agrarian Reading of the Bible* (Cambridge: Cambridge University Press, 2008), 122–23.

11 James Luther Mays, *Micah*, Old Testament Library (Philadelphia: Westminster Press, 1976), 64.

12 Gunther H. Wittenberg, "The Vision of Land in Jeremiah 32," in *The Earth Story in the Psalms and the Prophets*, ed. Norman C. Habel (Sheffield, England: Sheffield Academic, 2001), 136.

13 Wittenberg, 141–42.

14 Elaine M. Wainwright, *Habitat, Human, and Holy: An Eco-rhetorical Reading of the Gospel of Matthew* (Sheffield, England: Sheffield Phoenix, 2017), 198.

15 Wainwright, 198–99.

16 Sigve K. Tonstad, *The Letter to the Romans: Paul among the Ecologists* (Sheffield, England: Sheffield Phoenix, 2017), 260.

17 James Limburg, "Down-to-Earth Theology: Psalm 104 and the Environment," *Currents in Theology and Mission* 21, no. 5 (October 1994): 346.

CHAPTER 4

1 Bob Smietana, "How a Group of Refugees Saved a Church on the Brink of Collapsing," *Washington Post*, August 18, 2017, https://tinyurl.com/jhb42cb9.

2 Walter Brueggemann, *The Prophetic Imagination*, 2nd ed. (Minneapolis: Augsburg Fortress, 2001), 64–65.

3 Thomas Groome, *Sharing Faith: A Comprehensive Approach to Religious Education and Pastoral Ministry; The Way of Shared Praxis* (Eugene, OR: Wipf & Stock, 1991), 266.

4 Sample, *Ministry in an Oral Culture*, 29–44.

5 "COP24: Global Church Bodies Urge Transformative Action to Protect the Most Vulnerable," United Nations Office for the Coordination of Humanitarian Affairs, accessed December 3, 2018, https://tinyurl.com/wpa9fh7j.

6 An excellent overview of this system and the disadvantages it presents for farmers can be found in Sally Lee and Marcello Cappellazzi, dirs., *Under Contract: Farmers and the Fine Print* (Pittsboro, NC: Rural Advancement Foundation International-USA, 2016).

7 "About," Trickle Bee Café, accessed June 28, 2018, http://tricklebeecafe.org.

CHAPTER 5

1 P. R. Shukla et al., eds., *Climate Change and Land: An IPCC Special Report on Climate Change, Desertification, Land Degradation, Sustainable Land Management, Food Security, and Greenhouse Gas Fluxes in Terrestrial Ecosystems*, IPCC, 2019, https://www.ipcc.ch/srccl/.

2 *The State of Food Security and Nutrition in the World 2020: Transforming Food Systems for Affordable Healthy Diets*, FAO, IFAD, UNICEF, WFP, and WHO, last updated August 12, 2020, http://www.fao.org/3/ca9692en/online/ca9692en.html#.

3 D. R. Reidmiller et al., eds., *Fourth National Climate Assessment*, vol. 2, *Impacts, Risks, and Adaptation in the United States* (Washington, DC: USGCRP, 2018), https://doi.org/10.7930/NCA4.2018.

4 Reidmiller et al.

5 Reidmiller et al.

6 "About," Food and Water Watch, accessed August 10, 2020, https://www.foodandwaterwatch.org/about.

7 Maria Cristina Rulli, Antonio Saviori, and Paolo D'Odorico, "Global Land and Water Grabbing," *PNAS* 110, no. 3 (2013): 892–97, https://doi.org/10.1073/pnas.1213163110.

8 Brian Bienkowski, "Corporations Grabbing Land and Water Overseas," *Scientific American*, February 12, 2013, https://www.scientificamerican.com/article/corporations-grabbing-land-and-water-overseas/.

9 Marianne Goodland, "Buying and Drying: Water Lessons from Crowley County," *Colorado Independent*, July 9, 2015, https://www.coloradoindependent.com/2015/07/09/buying-and-drying-water-lessons-from-crowley-county/.

10 Jean-Daniel Collomb, "The Ideology of Climate Change Denial in the United States," *European Journal of American Studies* 9, no. 1 (2014), http://journals.openedition.org/ejas/10305.

11 "Scientific Consensus: Earth's Climate Is Warming," Earth Science Communications Team, NASA's Jet Propulsion Laboratory, last updated August 25, 2020, https://climate.nasa.gov/scientific-consensus/.

12 "Food and Climate Change," Johns Hopkins University Center for a Livable Future, accessed August 10, 2020, http://www.foodsystemprimer.org/food-production/food-and-climate-change/.

13 "Global Warming of 1.5 °C," IPCC, accessed August 10, 2020, https://www.ipcc.ch/sr15/.

14 "Record-Breaking Atlantic Hurricane Season Draws to an End," NOAA, November 24, 2020, updated June 10, 2021, https://www.noaa.gov/media-release/record-breaking-atlantic-hurricane-season-draws-to-end.

15 Wendell Berry, *The Unsettling of America: Culture and Agriculture* (New York: Random House, 1978), 198 (emphasis added).

16 Roger Cohn, "Wendell Berry: A Strong Voice for Local Farming and the Land," *YaleEnvironment360*, Yale School of the Environment, March 6, 2013, https://e360.yale.edu/features/interview_wendell_berry_a_strong_voice_for_local_farming_and_the_land.

17 David W. Orr, *Hope Is an Imperative: The Essential David Orr* (Washington, DC: Island Press, 2011), xix.

18 Orr, 326, 332 (emphasis added).
19 *Merriam-Webster,* s.v. "narrative," accessed August 11, 2020, https://www.merriam-webster.com/dictionary/narrative.
20 Sample, *Ministry in an Oral Culture,* 5, 30.
21 "In U.S., Decline of Christianity Continues at Rapid Pace: An Update on America's Changing Religious Landscape," Pew Research Center, October 17, 2019, https://www.pewforum.org/2019/10/17/in-u-s-decline-of-christianity-continues-at-rapid-pace/.
22 Margaret Myers, "These Are the 5 Causes Millennials Care about the Most," Renewal Project, October 12, 2017, https://tinyurl.com/db8rbmha; Caitlin Fairchild, "These Are the Causes Gen Z Cares about the Most," Renewal Project, June 26, 2019, https://www.therenewalproject.com/these-are-the-causes-gen-z-cares-about-the-most/.
23 "Transcript: Greta Thunberg's Speech at the U.N. Climate Action Summit," NPR, September 23, 2019, https://tinyurl.com/mjr9nuk6.
24 "Young People Are Boosting Global Climate Action," United Nations Climate Change, August 12, 2020, https://unfccc.int/news/young-people-are-boosting-global-climate-action.
25 Gerard O'Connell, "Pope Francis: The Pandemic Has 'Given us a Chance to Develop New Ways of Living,'" *America: The Jesuit Review,* September 1, 2020, https://tinyurl.com/26xxpmwe.

RECOMMENDED RESOURCES

Berry, Wendell. *The Unsettling of America: Culture and Agriculture.* Reprint ed. Berkeley, CA: Counterpoint, 2015.

    Berry is an essential read in the arena of sustainable agriculture and its necessity for society. Written in 1977, just prior to the 1980s farm crisis, this book was prophetic then and continues to be absolutely relevant. This is evidenced by the fact of its many subsequent editions and reprintings. I also recommend Berry's collection of essays *Bringing It to the Table: On Farming and Food* (Berkeley, CA: Counterpoint, 2009).

Davis, Ellen F. *Scripture, Culture, and Agriculture: An Agrarian Reading of the Bible.* Cambridge: Cambridge University Press, 2008.

    This is one of the best biblical commentaries on the intersection of the socioeconomics of agriculture and the biblical tradition. Davis brings her Old Testament scholarship into conversation with Wendell Berry's reflections on land and culture.

Fick, Gary W. *Food, Farming, and Faith.* SUNY Series on Religion and the Environment. Albany, NY: SUNY Press, 2008.

    Fick is a professor of agronomy at Cornell University and a Christian. This thoughtful book integrates science and faith around the issues of the land and growing food.

Hauter, Wenonah. *Foodopoly: The Battle over the Future of Food and Farming in America*. New York: New Press, 2012.

Hauter is the founder and executive director of Food and Water Watch, an NGO based in Washington, DC, that I reference in chapter 5. This book is an excellent treatment of the concerns over consolidation and globalization in the food system and alternatives to that system.

Jung, L. Shannon. *Food for Life: The Spirituality and Ethics of Eating*. Minneapolis: Augsburg Fortress, 2004.

Jung has written a wonderful trilogy of books focused on food, ethics, and spirituality that includes *Sharing Food: Christian Practices for Enjoyment* (Minneapolis: Fortress Press, 2006) and *Hunger and Happiness: Feeding the Hungry, Nourishing Our Souls* (Minneapolis: Augsburg Fortress, 2009). If you are going to pick one, choose *Food for Life*, which more closely relates to the topic of this book and also includes a reflection on the food philosophy of Shalom Hill Farm, the rural education and retreat center I founded.

Mays, James Luther, Patrick D. Miller, and Paul J. Achtemeier, eds. *Interpretation: A Bible Commentary for Teaching and Preaching*. Louisville: Westminster John Knox, 2012.

The *Interpretation* series is an excellent resource for both preaching and teaching. Volumes are based on sound scholarship but are written in an accessible manner with less emphasis on technical terminology and more stress on practical application. Walter Brueggemann's *Genesis*, Patrick Miller's

Deuteronomy, and James Limburg's *Hosea—Micah* are particularly strong in the area of care of creation. Miller and Limburg refer specifically to issues that pertain to a rural setting. These are a must for someone serving in a small-town and rural setting.

Orr, David W. *Hope Is an Imperative: The Essential David Orr.* Washington, DC: Island Press, 2011.

This collection of essays is uncompromisingly honest about the current realities of climate change and its danger to environmental sustainability. At the same time, it inspires perseverance in its call to hope "with its sleeves rolled up."

Sample, Tex. *Ministry in an Oral Culture: Living with Will Rogers, Uncle Remus, and Minnie Pearl.* Louisville: Westminster John Knox, 1994.

Though just over a quarter of a century old, this book is still the best on ministry in a small-town and rural context. It is an engaging read based on solid research and Sample's own ministry experience.

Schut, Michael, ed. *Food and Faith: Justice, Joy and Daily Bread.* New York: Morehouse, 2009.

This fascinating collection of essays by various contributors reflects on food and eating and how they shape a Christian ecological ethic. The book comes with a study guide that can be used for group reflection.

Wirzba, Norman. *Food and Faith: A Theology of Eating.* 2nd ed. Cambridge: Cambridge University Press, 2019.

Wirzba is one of the leading thinkers on the nexus of Christian ethics, care of creation, and climate change, and this is his best book thus far on that topic.

WORD & WORLD BOOKS

THEOLOGY FOR CHRISTIAN MINISTRY

Informing and inspiring Christian leaders and communities to proclaim God's *Word* to a *World* God created and loves. Articulating the fullness of both realities and the creative intersection between them.

Word & World Books is a partnership between Luther Seminary, the board of the periodical *Word & World*, and Fortress Press.

Books in the series include:

Rooted and Renewing: Imagining the Church's Future in Light of Its New Testament Origins by Troy M. Troftgruben (2019)

Journeying in the Wilderness: Forming Faith in the 21st Century by Terri Martinson Elton (2020)

God So Enters into Relationships That . . . . : A Biblical View by Terence E. Fretheim (2020)

Today Everything Is Different: An Adventure in Prayer and Action by Dirk G. Lange (2021)

Life Unsettled: A Scriptural Journey for Wilderness Times by Cory Driver (2021)

Everyone Must Eat: Food, Sustainability, and Ministry by Mark L. Yackel-Juleen (2021)